THE ￼PIRITUAL POWER

OF A MOTHER

ENCOURAGEMENT FOR THE HOMESCHOOLING MOM

THE SPIRITUAL POWER

OF A MOTHER

MICHAEL P. FARRIS

BROADMAN
& HOLMAN
PUBLISHERS

NASHVILLE, TENNESSEE

0–8054–2599–3

Published by Broadman & Holman Publishers
Nashville, Tennessee

Subject Heading: HOMESCHOOLING
Dewey Decimal Classification: 649

Unless otherwise noted, Scripture quotations are from the Holy
Bible, New International Version, copyright © 1973, 1978, 1984 by
International Bible Society. Quotations identified NASB are from the
New American Standard Bible, © the Lockman Foundation, 1960, 1962,
1963, 1968, 1971, 1972, 1973, 1975, 1977; used by permission. Quotations
identified NKJV are from the New King James Version, copyright ©
1979, 1980, 1982, Thomas Nelson, Inc., Publishers.

1 2 3 4 5 7 8 9 10 07 07 06 05 04 03

CONTENTS

Preface   vii

1. The Spiritual Power of a Mother   1
2. Baby Love   25
3. Christy's Graduation   29
4. The Hard Days   33
5. Homier Than Thou   37
6. Thanks, Mom   41
7. Advantages of Older Kids Teaching Younger Kids   45
8. God Writes Our Children's Stories   49
9. The Dangerous Myth of the Perfect Homeschool Mom   53
10. End-of-the-Year Blues   71
11. God Uses Temporal Needs to Achieve Spiritual Results   73
12. Summer School   77
13. Eternal Perspective Makes Priorities Clearer   81
14. The Dangers of Playing with Romance   85
15. Self-esteem and Achievement   89
16. The Conspiracy against Church and Decency   93
17. How Can I Follow If My Husband Won't Lead?   97

PREFACE

In my vocation, my first priority is the kingdom of God, and my second priority is America. I want to advance both priorities.

After twenty years in the homeschooling movement, I have become absolutely convinced that one of the best things I can do for both the kingdom of God and for America is to encourage homeschooling moms.

Christian homeschooling has a great academic reputation that is fully deserved, but its real impact will clearly be in the spiritual realm. Homeschooling is the ultimate tool for discipleship. You can fake spirituality in Sunday school and church. It is impossible to fake it at home on a sustained basis.

Children who are homeschooling have the opportunity for a life-changing form of spiritual training that will impact their own lives and the lives of countless others they touch.

If a mom stops homeschooling, such an impact will be diminished substantially in most cases.

Homeschooling moms are also doing more to change the face of American politics and culture than any other single group. The biggest problem in Washington, D.C., is that our leaders don't have a clear understanding of the purposes of government. Most don't understand that neither God nor the Constitution expected government to be the human institution to save mankind from all of its sorrows and woes. Government was expected to protect life, liberty, and property. When government tries to be a mini-Messiah, our freedom and our fortunes are put in grave jeopardy.

The best way to change this problem is to raise up a generation of children who do not believe that government should pretend to be a mini-Messiah.

When children get their education from the government, that is a difficult task. But when children get their education from their mothers, they have the ability to understand the world from the same perspective as our founding fathers.

Even if homeschooling mothers never said a word to their children about politics, by simply providing their own children an education at home, they have made it possible for their children to deeply embrace our nation's foundational principles of freedom.

After this preface, I am not going to say another word about politics in this book. The goal of this book is to encourage homeschooling mothers. But I wanted to begin my encouragement with this perspective.

Mom, you may think you are just involved in academic instruction with a little bit of spirituality thrown in from time to time. You understand how hard the effort can be, but you probably don't understand the grand scope of the reward that is coming through your efforts.

You need a bigger perspective.

This book is written as my wife Vickie is beginning our family's twenty-first year of homeschooling. (Some of the chapters in the book were written in the past and are dated accordingly.)

From our long-range vantage point we can see the huge benefits (spiritual and academic) that homeschooling has produced in the lives of our children as they have matured and gone on to adulthood. But I also want you to see the big picture that I see from my office as the founder of Home School Legal Defense Association and the president of Patrick Henry College.

By teaching your children at home, you are sowing the fields that will produce a crop of freedom-loving citizens who are essential if America and the free world are to survive. If people do not believe the principles of freedom, they will not remain free.

Mom, I want you to be encouraged because I want you to continue sowing this seed.

You cannot be encouraged if I deviate one degree from the truth. The truth is that homeschooling is hard work. But the bigger truth is that there are great rewards.

Come, let's look together at the issues that concern moms. Let's get perspective. Let's see the rewards that lie ahead.

Homeschooling moms are willing to work hard if someone can just assure them that the efforts are worth it.

If you want someone to tell you how to do the details, this isn't the book. No guilt trips. No to-do lists. No formulas.

But if you want to be encouraged so that you have the strength to keep going, you've come to the right place. I hope to point you to God within the real context of the daily life of a homeschooling mom.

You're doing incredibly important things. I know it's hard. But the rewards for you, for your children, for your nation, and for the kingdom of God are very, very real.

THE SPIRITUAL POWER OF A MOTHER

The feminist movement strives for power. Feminist ideology preaches the acquisition of power for essentially self-centered purposes—career, control of "one's own body," politics, cash.

A mother's power is premised on the opposite of selfishness. A new life is born out of nine months of discomfort and sacrifice and not a little pain. That new life is nurtured and guided through sleepless nights and endless days. The delivery may have ended in the hospital, but a mother continues in labor for years afterward as she continues to sacrifice the best hours of her day and the best years of her life for the good of her children.

The feminist ideology can never truly compete with godly motherhood in the acquiring of power. Ultimately, power is the ability to influence the decisions and actions of other people. Few people will be willing to follow a leader committed to selfishness.

Ultimately, that leader will prove her commitment to the view that "I come first" and leave her followers in a compromised position. We trust a leader who sacrificially demonstrates his or her commitment to our well-being, for we are willingly guided by a person who genuinely loves us.

We have all heard the saying, "The hand that rocks the cradle rules the world." This is true for one simple reason: sacrificial love is inherently more trustworthy than selfishness. This is why godly mothers will always have greater influence than secular feminists.

I would like for us to consider four aspects of a mother's power over the lives of her children from examples of motherhood we find in Scripture. It is my fervent hope that these examples will both encourage you and invigorate you to do an even better job with your children. But don't expect me to give you too many lists of goals to accomplish or tasks to complete. Sometimes such lists get in the way of seeing the big picture. And this is definitely a "big picture" kind of book.

I believe that the most important thing I can do for mothers is to help them see the long-term positive impact they are having in the lives of their children. It is from gaining that "big picture" perspective that we find deep encouragement. And after twenty years in the homeschooling movement, I am convinced that the number-one need of moms is encouragement to get through the days and nights of labor and sacrifice that we call motherhood.

The Power of a Mother's Prayer: The Story of Hannah

Samuel was a great man of God whose life was extraordinarily shaped by his mother's prayers. His very birth was an answer to his mother's prayer.

It is interesting to note that Samuel's father appeared to accept the fact that his wife Hannah would not have children. Now it is true that Elkanah had two wives and the other had given him several children. Although he dearly loved Hannah and probably wanted to have children with her as well, he was content with the situation as it was.

Hannah was not content and took her desire for children to the Lord. She prayed earnestly, not just for a child but for a son.

In bitterness of soul Hannah wept much and prayed to the Lord.

> And she made a vow, saying, "O LORD Almighty, if
> you will only look upon your servant's misery and
> remember me, and not forget your servant but give her
> a son, then I will give him to the LORD for all the days
> of his life, and no razor will ever be used on his head"
> (1 Samuel 1:10–11).

Samuel was conceived and born because God answered this prayer of his mother. Not only was Samuel born as a result of his mother's prayer, but his life was ordered and shaped in direct response to her prayers as well.

Hannah vowed in prayer to the Lord that Samuel would be set apart, a Nazarite, in service to God. In her first prayer, Hannah committed her son to this special order of service that is implicit in the statement, "No razor shall ever be used on his head." (When I was in high school in the late 1960s, I asked my mother why she didn't pray that for me so I could have long hair. She would laugh and tell me that I still had to get a haircut.)

But Hannah followed through with her initial prayer, fulfilling her promise while continuing to pray: Samuel's parents brought the boy to Eli, and said to him,

As surely as you live, my lord, I am the woman who stood here beside you praying to the Lord. I prayed for this child, and the Lord has granted me what I asked of him. So now I give him to the Lord. For his whole life he will be given over to the Lord." And he worshiped the Lord there (1 Samuel 1:25–28).

Consider this incredibly simple but important truth about Samuel: Samuel served God because of his mother's prayer.

Hannah's prayers were the central factor in both his birth and his beginning a life in God's service. But that influence did not cease when Hannah left her beloved son in the house of Eli.

Consider the lengthy prayer of Hannah recorded in 1 Samuel 2: 1–10:

Then Hannah prayed and said:

"My heart rejoices in the LORD;
   in the LORD my horn is lifted high.
My mouth boasts over my enemies,
   for I delight in your deliverance.

"There is no one holy like the LORD;
   there is no one besides you;
   there is no Rock like our God.

"Do not keep talking so proudly
   or let your mouth speak such arrogance,
for the LORD is a God who knows,
   and by him deeds are weighed.

"The bows of the warriors are broken,
   but those who stumbled are armed with strength.

Those who were full hire themselves out for food,
   but those who were hungry hunger no more.

She who was barren has borne seven children,
   but she who has had many sons pines away.

"The Lord brings death and makes alive;
   he brings down to the grave and raises up.
The Lord sends poverty and wealth;
   he humbles and he exalts.
He raises the poor from the dust
   and lifts the needy from the ash heap;
he seats them with princes
   and has them inherit a throne of honor.

"For the foundations of the earth are the Lord's;
   upon them he has set the world.
He will guard the feet of his saints,
   but the wicked will be silenced in darkness.

"It is not by strength that one prevails;
   those who oppose the Lord will be shattered.
He will thunder against them from heaven;
   the Lord will judge the ends of the earth.

"He will give strength to his king
   and exalt the horn of his anointed."

As I was studying this prayer, a question popped into my head: *How did this prayer get recorded in the Bible?* Undoubtedly, Samuel was the source of this prayer in the book that bears his name. But how would a boy who had just been weaned remember a prayer like this? Samuel didn't write down the prayer when he was a little child. He would have recorded it much later in life.

Now, let me be clear. I firmly believe in the inspiration of Scripture. The Holy Spirit has more than enough power to have supernaturally revealed the content of Hannah's prayer to Samuel decades after she had prayed it. But my educated guess is that this is not the method that God used in this particular case. I believe that Hannah taught this prayer to her son in a method that caused him to remember it for his whole life.

I saw how this could have been done by watching my wife Vickie's interaction with our tenth child, Peter.

When Peter was a toddler, he liked Vickie to sing to him as she put him to bed. Sometimes I would sing to him as well. I would sing a variety of songs, but Vickie regularly sang a song that quickly became Peter's favorite. He called it "Gloria." (It wasn't the rock song from the 1960s by that name.) Vickie was singing "Angels We Have Heard on High," and Peter dubbed it "Gloria" because of the repetition of that word in the refrain.

She began singing that song around Christmas one year and carried it on for months afterward because Peter liked it so much. But after a while, Peter stopped asking for "Gloria" so often, and he heard it less and less.

The following Christmas, when Peter was not quite three years old, we sang "Angels We Have Heard On High" in church. Peter, who knew the words to only a few songs, sang all four verses of this great carol from memory. Vickie had burned this song into our little boy's memory by constant repetition in the months past.

Hannah may very well have done something similar with Samuel. As she prepared for the day when she would leave her son at the house of Eli, Hannah may have begun to pray this prayer for her son. Then she may have prayed it again. And again. Until it became a habit, perhaps a nighttime ritual that mothers often do with their children as they put them to bed. And like Peter, Samuel may have had this prayer burned into his memory by his mother's constant repetition.

Another possibility is that Hannah wrote this prayer down for her son. She may have said something like this as she was getting ready to leave her son at Eli's: "Samuel, there are going to be times when you are at Eli's house that you may miss me. I am going to miss you every single day. When you miss me and want to know my heart for you, read this prayer that I have written for you. It expresses my heart and my love for you, my son."

Whichever way it was, it appears that Samuel knew this prayer from his mother word for word later in life when it came time to record the events in this book.

Several things contained in this prayer are worthy of closer examination. First, from this prayer Samuel learned that he was an answer to prayer. He learned that God had specially created him. And he learned that his mother felt exalted as a result of his birth.

Think of the effect on a child who hears his mother praying, "O Lord, thank you for exalting me by giving me my son or my daughter."

Samuel also learned from this prayer that God fights for those who trust in Him. Again, think of the lifelong influence on the child who hears his mother pray and then sees God answer her prayer.

On the very first day our family began homeschooling in September 1982, Vickie prayed a special prayer with our three little girls. She prayed, "God, I ask You to use our homeschooling in a way that will allow us to share the gospel with other people."

Just before lunch, our doorbell rang. Two Jehovah's Witnesses were standing there eager to tell our family about their doctrine. Vickie had other plans. She invited them in, listened patiently, and then shared the gospel in clear terms.

Our girls watched all of this. Their mother had prayed for a chance to share the gospel, and not two hours later they witnessed the answer to that prayer.

If our girls had been off at school, perhaps they would have been pleased to hear how God had answered their mother's prayer when they got home. But there was doubtless a far greater impact on their lives from actually watching God's answer to prayer unfold before their eyes.

Indeed, this encouraged both Vickie and me that we had made the right decision to homeschool our children. On the very first day, we saw the potential to impact the development of our children's faith by having them with us as we endeavored to live a life of faith.

Children who witness God's answers to their mother's prayers are quickly placed on the path of spiritual growth and maturity.

Hannah's prayer impacted Samuel not only when he was a child. When he was well into his years of adult ministry, God called upon Samuel to anoint Saul as the first king of Israel. I can imagine Samuel's thoughts as he was walking toward Gilgal to anoint Saul. Suddenly, the words of his mother's prayer may have echoed in his mind.

. . . those who oppose the LORD will be shattered.

He will thunder against them from heaven;
    the LORD will judge the ends of the earth.
He will give strength to his king
    and exalt the horn of his anointed.

When Hannah prayed these words, there was no king in Israel. No one had been anointed for such a purpose. God moved Hannah to pray prophetically over her son in a way that had a clear influence on the life of the nation of Israel.

Samuel had to be deeply touched and perhaps amazed as he reflected on the lifelong impact of his mother's prayer on his own life and, indeed, upon all Israel.

Moms, I know I don't have to tell you to pray for your children. It would be like saying, "Mom, remember to breathe. It's really important." You pray for your children. Perhaps you could pray a little more often, but you pray.

I want to encourage you to see the impact you can have on the whole life of your child through prayer. Just as you prayed for your children while you carried them inside you, continue to pray for your children's future dedication to God and service for God.

God is especially pleased to answer such prayers. Our nation and our world need mighty men and women of God who, like Samuel, will lead our nation in righteousness. Whether such leaders will arise may largely be a matter of how many mothers beseech the Lord in earnest prayer that their sons and daughters will become great men and women of God.

And, moms, make sure that your children know your prayers. Maybe you will want to do something like what Hannah may have done. Take the time to write down a special prayer for your children and give it to them. Maybe you could write it down in the inside cover of your child's Bible. (Keep a copy; kids have a habit of losing things.)

The power of such prayers over your child cannot possibly be overstated. The day will come when your son or daughter will see the hand of God and say in amazement, "*This* is what my mother was praying about years and years ago."

Your prayers have power because they mingle your love with the even greater love of your child's Heavenly Father.

The Power of a Mother's Protection: The Story of Jochebed

Moses was destined for death. But his mother looked at her baby and saw that he was a fine child. And she did what was in her power to protect her son from death.

Now, every mother believes her child is fine; in fact most mothers believe that their children are perfect. At least until they become teenagers.

I have heard many different politicians tell the same joke after they have received a flowery introduction. "I wish my parents could have been here to hear that," they say. "My father would have enjoyed it, and my mother would have believed it."

Mothers believe in their children. They particularly believe good things about their children's future.

There is no doubt that my mother's extraordinary optimism toward me and my future had a profound effect in making me willing to try new paths that some considered risky.

I believe there is a profound truth hidden in this observation that Jochebed made concerning Moses. Mothers look at their children through the eyes of love that project a great future for their child and pronounce it all "fine." It is a God-given instinct that causes a mother to feel this way about her child. And this instinct creates the equally God-given desire to protect her child because she sees the great potential that lies under that little helpless exterior. She instinctively knows that her child cannot reach his or her potential without her protection.

All Christian moms are accused at times of being too protective of their children. This charge is leveled at homeschooling moms fairly frequently.

Mom, don't let the hecklers get you down. Your protective instinct comes from God.

Now, I have heard a few people—very few—advocate a form of child rearing that I feel goes a little too far. They say that foolishness is bound up in the heart of a child, and, of course, this is correct. But they take that to mean that their children should never play with another child unless they are personally present to prevent any foolishness.

By this standard your own children couldn't play with their siblings. If you want to protect your child from any unsupervised exposure to foolishness, you could never leave two brothers alone even for five minutes.

But this kind of thinking is very, very rare. Almost all homeschooling families have a more realistic understanding of child rearing, yet are far more protective of their children than the world around them.

Studies show that 98 percent of homeschool children are involved in two or more outside activities each week, activities such as scouting, sports, ballet, or church youth groups.

But consider two statistics that reflect the protective attitude of most homeschooling families. Sixty-two percent of the children in public school watch three or more hours of television daily. Ninety-four percent of homeschooled children watch less than three hours of television daily.

There is good reason to protect your child from the wickedness that dominates television. Children who hear God's name repeatedly taken in vain have a difficult time holding God in high esteem. Mothers, protect your children from profanity! Children accustomed to seeing sexual immorality on television, in movies, or in magazines will have a hard time adhering to God's standards in this area. Mothers, protect your children from such illicit behavior!

In the early 1980s, when I was the general counsel for Concerned Women for America, I represented a woman named Betty Batey.

Betty had married Frank after the two had met through the church in which they were both active members. They had a son named Brian. But not too long after Brian's birth, Betty discovered that Frank had a past, and a present, practice of homosexuality. After she confronted Frank, he divorced her.

Not too surprisingly, the judge in San Diego County awarded custody to Betty. Frank got visitation rights.

By the time Brian was eight or nine years old, he didn't want to visit his father anymore. Although there was no evidence that Brian was physically molested, he was simply uncomfortable in the sinfulness that was overtly practiced in his father's home. And although Betty didn't forbid him from visiting Frank, neither did she encourage it.

The San Diego judges didn't approve of Betty's approach. She was called into court again and again for contempt for refusing to send Brian on visitations.

Then came the unexpected ruling. A judge determined that if Betty wouldn't send Brian on visitation that she (the judge) would award custody to Frank. And that is just what she did. You can imagine how Betty felt at that point.

Frank had custody of Brian for one week when Betty got her first visitation. Betty took a rather extended "visitation" with her son. She loaded the car and left California and headed for rural Texas, where she and Brian spent eighteen wonderful months away from Frank and his sinful lifestyle.

Betty then heard a rumor that the FBI was looking for her. It was erroneous, but she panicked. She left Texas for Colorado and ended up in Denver where she was advised by a pastor of a large church of her denomination to turn herself in to the authorities. She was immediately jailed.

That is where I met her—at the jail in Denver.

Betty had been charged in California with a form of kidnapping known as "custodial interference." There was no realistic way to stop her from being returned to California for trial, so we agreed to her return so that we could battle the charges directly.

There were multiple phases of the case that arose from all this, two civil and one criminal.

In the civil trial, I called a Jewish child psychiatrist to testify about the effect of premature exposure to sexuality on children. I will never forget what he explained to the court.

His professional opinion was that men who are tempted by homosexuality develop this form of deviant thinking because of a premature and significant exposure to sex. This can come from being molested, from watching pornography, and even from early explicit sex education. He was very careful to say that not every boy who has one of these experiences becomes a homosexual, but every homosexual male has had some form of this exposure in his background. (This is like saying that not every smoker gets lung cancer, but we know that lung cancer is caused by smoking.)

Betty didn't know these studies, but she knew her mother's heart, and she wanted to protect her son from evil. There were various outcomes to the different phases of Betty's case, but the criminal trial had the most pertinent result.

At the end of the prosecutor's case, I moved to dismiss the charges because there was no proof that Betty had a criminal intent when she left California to go to Texas with her son. To everyone's astonishment the trial judge agreed saying that her only desire was to protect her son and *that* was not criminal intent. The charges were dismissed.

Mom, don't let anyone tell you that you should follow mainstream thinking. It is the little foxes that spoil the vines. The pound-pound-pound of cultural degradation that dominates entertainment and the world in its grasp leads to a "stress fracture" in the morality of too many children. Don't let your child's ability to stand tall be broken in this way.

Be careful of your children's associates. While no one is perfect and while it is neither possible nor necessarily desirable to keep your children away from nonbelievers, certain playmates are simply unacceptable because of their special proclivities toward evil.

It was hard for Jochebed to do what she had to do to protect her son's life. Nor was it easy for Betty Batey. Few moms will face such extreme situations as these mothers faced. But we all face an extremely degraded culture. Protection from the extremes that are too readily accepted by the world around us is a necessary reality for every mother who believes that her child is a fine child with a bright future.

The Power of a Mother's Teaching: The Story of Eunice

Timothy learned about God and developed his faith in Christ as a result of his mother's teaching: "I have been reminded of your sincere faith, which first lived in your grandmother Lois and in your mother Eunice and, I am persuaded, now lives in you also" (2 Timothy 1:5).

The Scriptures never specifically command mothers to teach their children. Fathers are commanded to teach their children in Ephesians 6:4. "Fathers, do not exasperate your children; instead, bring them up in the training and instruction of the Lord." Parents are commanded to teach their children to love God in Deuteronomy 6:1–7:

These are the commands, decrees and laws the LORD your God directed me to teach you to observe in the land that you are crossing the Jordan to possess, so that you, your children and their children after them may fear the LORD your God as long as you live by keeping all his decrees and commands that I give you, and so that you may enjoy long life. Hear, O Israel, and be careful to obey so that it may go well with you and that you may increase greatly in a land flowing with milk and honey, just as the LORD, the God of your fathers, promised you.

Hear, O Israel: The LORD our God, the LORD is one. Love the LORD your God with all your heart and with all your soul and with all your strength. These commandments that I give you today are to be upon your hearts. Impress them on your children. Talk about

them when you sit at home and when you walk along
the road, when you lie down and when you get up.

But mothers are never specifically singled out and commanded to teach their children. Scripture assumes that mothers
will teach their children, as is reflected in Proverbs 6:20:

My son, keep your father's commands
and do not forsake your mother's teaching.

All moms teach their children. But homeschooling moms take
an extraordinarily active role in teaching their children.

But I want all moms to remember that academics are not the
most important thing they teach their children. Academics are
important. But not the most important.

Moms are the best teachers of manners. Dads are usually
manners-impaired adults, at least by comparison. But, as important as politeness and orderliness can be, these are not the most
important truths a child will learn from his mother.

Motherly wisdom is also important but not the most important. Things like, "Don't keeping picking at that scab, or it will
never heal." Or, "Wear clean underwear in case you get in a
wreck." Your practical advice may have many important benefits,
but it is not the most important thing to teach your child.

Nor is teaching your child about God the most important
thing. (Follow what I am saying very carefully so that there will be
no misunderstanding.) Teaching about God is important, but the
most important thing you can teach your child is *to believe in God*.

In fact, a sequence of reasoning from this passage in
Deuteronomy has convinced Vickie and me that it is God's will for
us to homeschool our children. (This is how we read this passage
for us. I would urge you to consider my explanation of the passage
but reach your own conclusion.)

To be honest, I must admit that the Bible does not directly say, "Thou shalt teach thy children their history and mathematics at home." But we must not shrug off the implications of this passage from Deuteronomy.

Jesus told us that the command to love God pronounced here in Deuteronomy 6 is the most important command in Scripture. And God was extraordinarily concerned that this command would be a reality for generation after generation. On both sides of this command we find directives to parents to teach their children to love God, and God tells us how we are to do this. We are to teach these commands as we "talk about them when [we] sit at home and when [we] walk along the road, when [we] lie down and when [we] get up." We teach our children to love God through the course of everyday living by having them watch us and listen to us as we live a life of faith. This is God's ordained teaching method for obeying His most important command to parents: teach your children to love God.

How can we use God's method of teaching our children to love Him if they are away from us during the core portion of every day in some institutional school? Bringing academic instruction home makes it much easier to follow God's method of hour-by-hour instruction in how to love God.

We don't know what academic subjects, if any, Eunice taught to her son Timothy. But we do know that Timothy's faith first lived in his grandmother and then in his mother. It then lived in Timothy. A mother's faith in God can indeed be taught. Your faith can be taught. But it will be passed to your children mostly through your actions.

Spending time with your children throughout the day may be God's method, but what about the content of your teaching?

Moms, if you want your child to believe in God, live daily in faith.

Do you complain a lot? A mom who regularly complains about her circumstances teaches her child that God is inadequate to meet her needs. A mother with a positive outlook on life teaches her children her faith.

Do you resist or resent your husband's authority? A mom who chafes against the authorities in her life teaches her children that God's authority may also be resisted or resented. A mom living happily with her husband teaches her children to cling to her faith.

Do you speak disparagingly to your children?

A few summers ago, Vickie and I were flying back from Canada with two of our children. In the row behind us were two mothers, each with two children. The mothers struck up a conversation, a loud conversation that we couldn't help but hear.

After swapping vacation accounts, one mom said to the other (as loudly as ever), "You know what would be a real vacation! It would be to get away from these kids." Her children were right there!

Now, I don't fault a mom for thinking that kind of thought. Nor would I fault a mom for sharing such a thought with her friend while the two of them were on a walk alone. And I think it is a very good idea for husband and wife to have times alone away from their children. But it is utterly unacceptable to say such things in so sarcastic a manner in front of one's children.

Some words should never cross our lips, even in anger. Here is one example of a degrading attack that we should never utter: "I wish you had never been born."

Children who hear such things will have a hard time believing in a God who, they are taught, loves them unconditionally. It is fine to speak boldly against your child's sin. But never, never, never speak evil about your child's very existence, for this will set up a roadblock to your child's ever adopting your faith.

Children will learn from their mothers (and from their fathers). Will they learn to believe in the God you serve? Your teaching through actions and words to them will have a powerful, perhaps decisive impact on their faith.

The Power of a Mother to Lift Her Children Higher than Herself: The Stories of Tamar, Rahab, Ruth, and Bathsheba

We love to recite the verses: "All Scripture is given by inspiration of God, and is profitable for doctrine, for reproof, for correction, for instruction in righteousness, that the man of God may be complete, thoroughly equipped for every good work" (2 Timothy 3:16–17 NKJV).

But we neglect whole portions of the Word, even though we need its wisdom or insight. For example, we rarely consult genealogies for profound wisdom. But I believe one of the most important lessons for Christian women (and implicitly for men also) is found in Matthew's genealogy of Jesus (Matthew 1:2–16).

Although Jewish genealogies rarely mentioned women, Matthew lists four women among the ancestors of Christ. All four had some blot against them that might surprise us that they would be singled out from among all the ancestral women for special mention.

Tamar

Tamar's story, recorded in Genesis 38, begins in sadness. She was married to Judah's oldest son Er, whom God killed because of

19

his wickedness. Tamar's life in that marriage must have been unpleasant.

Then, as Jewish law required, she was given in marriage to Er's brother Onan. Onan was supposed to fulfill an obligation to his dead brother by conceiving a child with Tamar. He was quite willing to have relations with Tamar, but Scripture records that he "spilled his seed on the ground," and she obviously did not get pregnant. God killed Onan for his wickedness. Her life continued in turmoil and sorrow.

At last, Judah promised to give Tamar his son Shelah when he grew up. But Shelah came of age, and Judah broke his promise.

So Tamar took her desire for children into her own hands. She posed as a prostitute and enticed her father-in-law Judah into having relations with her. That is how she got pregnant with the ancestor of Jesus Christ.

It is a tale of desperation and multiple layers of sin, a tale that God inspired Matthew to single out for special mention in the genealogy of the Son of God.

Rahab the Harlot

Some would consider it surprising that a foreign harlot would be a central figure in one of the most common stories children hear in Sunday school. Yet when Rahab had the opportunity to help the people of God, she did so with a skill that would fit convincingly into any tale of military espionage. She believed that the God of Israel was the one true God, and she acted upon this belief. It is for this reason that she is listed in Hebrews 11 among the heroes of faith.

Rahab married Salmon, who is thought by some commentators to have been one of the Israeli spies she protected. Through this marriage Rahab became the mother of Boaz, the same Boaz who married Ruth. A harlot became the mother of a man who is known, according to one commentator, as "a model of piety, chastity, and generosity."

Rahab's past was long behind her. Not only did she see her own life turned around, but her belief in the one true God also led her child to reflect her new faith, not her old lifestyle. Rahab experienced a mighty transformation in her own life that impacted her child's future for good.

Ruth

No Jewish man should have married Ruth. Jews were forbidden from marrying women from Moab (see Genesis 28:1). Yet two Jewish men married her.

Her early married life quickly turned to sorrow as her husband died. Despite her mother-in-law's bitterness, she was attracted to the God of Israel and returned with Naomi to live among the Jews.

She was taken by Boaz as his wife after an incident that was rife with possibilities for sin, but both she and Boaz behaved with absolute purity.

A forbidden, foreign woman with every reason to be bitter, but who by choice lived with great faith in Israel, is one of only four women to be listed in the records of the birth of the Son of God.

Bathsheba

The fourth and final woman in Christ's genealogy is Bathsheba. She is famous for having committed adultery with David while she was still Uriah's wife. For a number of reasons, spiritual responsibility for this sin has to be laid at the feet of

David. But Bathsheba was not molested. She appears to have willingly committed adultery with the king. Accordingly, we have to say that she also sinned.

Bathsheba made a very unwise choice. But she became the mother of Solomon, the wisest man who ever lived.

The Lesson for Moms

These were the great, great grandmothers of the Son of God. A forbidden woman. Two prostitutes. An adultress. Yet two of their sons, Boaz and Solomon, achieved special distinction in their own right.

Many of you mothers here today wish you could have back certain periods of your life to live over. Perhaps it would be your teens or your early twenties. Or maybe there was a failed marriage in your thirties.

Whatever it is, I want you to remember that:

- Tamar, who degraded herself with her father-in-law, was in the line of Christ.
- Rahab, the harlot, was the mother of Boaz and in the line of Christ.
- Ruth, the foreigner, was in the line of Christ.
- Bathsheba, the adulteress, was in the line of Christ.

No matter where you started, if you have accepted Jesus as your Savior, you are a child of God. In effect, you are in the line of Christ.

Not only can your life be transformed, but your children can avoid some of the experiences you went through. By the power of God, your children can be raised up, they can go higher, they can achieve spiritual distinction, even if their mother was born or lived for a season on the wrong side of the tracks.

I once shared this lesson with some homeschooling moms in a southern state. Afterwards, one mom came up to me crying. She said this message was the first word of encouragement she had ever had on this particular subject.

She told me that while she was in college she had been a prostitute. She had accepted Christ, changed her life, gotten married, and had several daughters. But there is a teaching that is fairly common in certain evangelical circles that served as a constant source of fear and discouragement to her. This teaching is based on Exodus 20:5: "You shall not bow down to them or worship them; for I, the LORD your God, am a jealous God, punishing the children for the sin of the fathers to the third and fourth generation of those who hate me."

She had heard teaching that emphasized this verse and predicted great harm for children based on the past sins of their parents and other ancestors. (Sometimes this teaching encourages people to use certain formula-driven prayers, like some magical incantation, that are supposed to relieve us from the penalty imposed by this verse.)

She walked in fear believing that her daughters were doomed to repeat her sinful behavior in one form or another.

My message that day was the same that I deliver to you: this teaching misconstrues the whole counsel of God's Word and misses the central truth of the gospel: *Jesus forgives sin.* He forgives us from the penalty of sin, and He releases us from the power of sin.

Not only does the gospel repudiate the idea that our children are doomed if we have ever sinned, but the very next verse in Exodus even sets us on the right track! God says that He will show "love to a thousand [generations] of those who love me and keep my commandments" (Exodus 20:6).

If you as a parent continue to wallow in sin, there may indeed be consequences in the lives of your children. But if you give your heart to Jesus and love God, then you are on the generational track of receiving God's love for a thousand generations.

Who are you to curse your children if God has promised to show them (and the next 999 generations) His love?

And we have more than logic to prove that we have the right interpretation of this passage. Did God punish Rahab for three and four generations for her sin? No, her son was Boaz—the model of piety and chastity.

Moms, the listing of the great-grandmothers of Christ conclusively proves that God's redemptive power is stronger than your past.

Conclusion

God can overcome your yesterdays, even if the yesterday you need to overcome was literally yesterday. God can lift you and your children up by the power of Jesus Christ, who forgives sins and turns the worst sinners into glorious saints.

BABY LOVE

Summer 1997

As I write this, bleary-eyed in a sweatshirt and pajamas at my home computer, my wife, Vickie is upstairs trying to get our newborn son, Peter James, to go back to sleep. Vickie is even more tired than I am, because only she can get up with him during the watches of the night to nurse Peter.

Newborns are a lot of hard work. You'd think that I'd remember that since this is our tenth child. But I tend to forget the details as the months and years pass. There is always more work and sacrifice required than I remember.

About ten days before Peter was born, I spoke at the World Congress on Families in Prague, Czech Republic. On the panel with me was a pediatrician from Venezuela who said something very interesting.

"It's in the middle of the night when moms are so tired and must sacrifice so greatly for their babies that they first fall deeply in love with their child," she said.

"People who see your child during the daytime hours may admire your baby and think many kindly thoughts, but those that really love that child most deeply are the ones who have worked the hardest to care for and meet the needs of that baby."

We have all heard of the children in orphanages who suffer "detachment syndrome" because they are not held and cuddled. In short, these children suffer because no one loved them enough to care for them when it wasn't convenient.

The comment from the Venezuelan doctor caused me to think about homeschooling.

Homeschooling also requires a lot of hard work. It is not convenient to prepare lesson plans when you'd rather be reading "Drama in Real Life" in *Reader's Digest*. It is not easy to sit with your eight-year-old and try to drill math facts when you'd rather be working in your garden. Like a newborn, a homeschool student requires a lot of hard work on the part of moms and dads that is inconvenient and comes at a great sacrifice.

I have spoken at a number of homeschool graduations. Invariably one or more of the parents or students who speak on these occasions share that because of homeschooling they feel far closer to one another than they ever imagined.

Call it bonding. Call it love. Call it what you will. But the formula for closeness between a parent and a child doesn't really change as your child grows older. Time. Sacrifice. Hard work. Inconvenient hours.

The world about us thinks that love blossoms only when things are pleasant.

If you want a love that only blossoms, maybe there is some merit in this approach. But if you want a love that grows deep roots in your heart, roots that cannot be broken by the winds of change or trouble, then the old formula is the best. Time. Sacrifice. Hard work. Inconvenient hours.

Homeschooling gives us all a uniquely intense opportunity to fall deeply in love with our children, and they with us.

CHRISTY'S GRADUATION

June 1998

As I write this I am sitting beside a small indoor pool at the Fairfield Inn in Fairborn, Ohio. Five of our children are splashing and making a fair amount of noise. It's raining outside, and the kids seem glad that the pool is indoors so they won't get wet. Go figure.

We are in Ohio to watch our oldest daughter, Christy, graduate from Cedarville College.

The swimmers are ages eleven, nine, eight, six, and four.

I have to admit that I was much younger when Christy was four—I was eighteen years younger to be precise. I'm pretty sure that I had more energy back in those days. Probably less wisdom. But definitely more energy.

At times like these I am struck with the long-range nature of the commitment to parenthood. It is a task to be assumed with solemn resolve and profound gratefulness to God.

Homeschooling parents undertake the responsibility for raising children in a very comprehensive sense. And I want to take
this space to encourage you, just as I need to be encouraged, to per-
severe for the long haul.

A decision to homeschool is not a mere decision to deliver academic content with the tutorial method. It is a decision to invest
the essence of your life, your time, in the lives of your
children.

If homeschooling were only an academic system, my wife and
I would have probably quit before this, our sixteenth year. The
differences in test scores are not reason enough, standing alone, to
undertake all this work.

But when I consider the spiritual and moral character of my
three grown daughters and the tremendous opportunities for
interaction that Vickie and I have had with them, I have an
unshakable conviction that all the years and all the work are a
small investment compared to the rewards we have received.

Let me suggest three ideas to hang on to when times are challenging and you entertain those nagging doubts about whether
you should quit.

First, remember *parents can't quit.* You can never stop being
your child's parent. This will still be true when you are eighty and
your child is fifty. Some parents, particularly some dads, try to quit
by simply running away. But even this is not a resignation from
parenthood; it is simply a resignation from responsibility.

You have only one choice: will I be a responsible or an irresponsible parent? Homeschooling is a responsible choice, but it
takes diligence to exercise this choice in a responsible way.

You can't quit being a parent, and you shouldn't quit being a
responsible parent.

Second, remember that *you are raising adults, not children.* The point of parenthood, like the point of homeschooling, is to bring your children to maturity. It is not enough to make a good start. Your parenthood will be judged by your finish, not your beginning.

I will admit that neither of these two thoughts will make the job of homeschooling easier. But my goal is to make quitting more difficult.

Third, we need to remember that *God will reward our meager efforts to exercise the self-discipline it takes to be a responsible parent with bounty that is out of proportion to our work.* But the rewards do not come overnight.

Consider two passages: Hebrews 12:11–12 teaches the need for perseverance as a condition of receiving a godly reward: "No discipline seems pleasant at the time, but painful. Later on, however, it produces a harvest of righteousness and peace for those who have been trained by it. Therefore, strengthen your feeble arms and weak knees."

And, one of my favorite verses, Isaiah 40:31, teaches the principle of the disproportionality of God's reward: "Yet those who wait for the LORD will gain new strength; they will mount up with wings like eagles, they will run and not get tired, they will walk and not become weary" (NASB).

All we do is wait upon the Lord, and we end up with wings like eagles.

As I reflect on the milestone of Christy's graduation, I know that Vickie and I have flown with eagles' wings many times to have come this far. And as I hear the din of our five little swimmers, I know with confident relief that those wings from God will be there again and again to carry all of us above and through the storms of life.

THE HARD DAYS

Some homeschool seminars would like to make you believe that every day is all sweetness and light, complete with joyful children who complete their assignments with enough time left over to help mom with the dishes. That is the homeschool equivalent of selling you the Brooklyn Bridge.

Some days just aren't like this. Some days, indeed some years, are just plain hard. Let me try to use a fun method to convey a serious point.

Even though America is plagued with an overabundance of top-ten lists, let me share my homeschool variation on this theme. And since homeschooling is at least twice as much fun as the alternatives, here are *The Top Twenty Advantages of Homeschooling* (forgetting passé advantages like achievement test scores).

20. Your kids never tell you that their teacher is smarter than you are.

19. If you can't find matching socks for your child first thing in the morning, who cares?

18. You never have to cancel school for snow days.

17. Your kids have good reason to think they might get spanked in school but no reason to think they might get shot.

16. If the principal gives the teacher a bad evaluation, she can stick her icy feet against his legs at night.

15. You can post the Ten Commandments on your school-room wall without getting sued.

14. You never have to drive your child's forgotten lunch to school.

13. Your child will never go to their twentieth high school reunion, meet an old flame, and recklessly abandon his marriage.

12. You get to change more than their diapers. You get to change their minds.

11. Your child never brings the flu home from school.

10. It's better to be a little concerned about socialization rather than really concerned about socialism.

9. When your children talk about New Age issues, they are referring to their birthday party.

8. Since becoming a homeschooling mom, you now have the legal right to throw a blunt kitchen object (slightly grazing, but not bruising, your husband's forehead) if he ever asks, "Why is dinner late?"

7. You never have to face the dilemma of whether to take your child's side or the teacher's side in a dispute at school.

6. If your child gets drugs at school it's probably Tylenol.

5. The teacher gets to kiss the principal in the faculty lounge and no one gossips.

4. Your kids recognize that this list is numerically in reverse order.

3. *Your* honor student can actually read the bumper sticker that you have on your car.

2. If your child claims that the dog ate his homework, you can ask the dog.

1. Some day your children will consider you to be a miracle-working expert and will turn to you for advice.

HOMIER THAN THOU

The apostle Paul wrote to the Philippians: "If anyone else thinks he has reason to put confidence in the flesh, I have more: circumcised on the eighth day, of the people of Israel, of the tribe of Benjamin, a Hebrew of Hebrews; in regard to the law, a Pharisee; as for zeal, persecuting the church; as for legalistic righteousness, faultless" (Philippians 3:4–6).

Listen to my own analogous "brag-list pedigree": My wife and I have ten children; we have been homeschooling since 1982; we are committed to courtship, have trained our children in citizenship and preparation for marriage; we are deeply involved in our local church (almost all children in our church are homeschooled); we welcome apprenticeship over college in many circumstances; and we drive only American cars.

There is an attitude that I see a little too often in the homeschooling movement that I call the "homier than thou" attitude. There used to be so few homeschoolers that the mere fact that you were homeschooling gave you spiritual bragging rights. Today there are so many homeschoolers out there that we have resorted to spiritual one-upmanship.

This is how the "homier than thou" attitude works. "Homeschooling is good, but the *really* great homeschoolers do _____." A myriad of bragging points can be used to fill in this blank: really great homeschoolers do unit study, or use a certain brand of curriculum, or belong to a certain national or local training program, or study classical literature, or bake their own bread, or do home births, or refuse vaccinations, or refuse social security numbers, or do not participate in church youth groups, or do not own a television, or do not use birth control, or . . . The potential list is endless.

My point is not to condemn any of these approaches to homeschooling or to training our children. My wife and I are fully committed to many of these "bragging points." What I hope to avoid for myself is the attitude of being "homier than thou."

Vickie and I may be more experienced homeschoolers because we have done this since 1982, but we are not necessarily better at it than someone who has done this for one or two years. We certainly have special challenges with ten children, but it is still a very challenging undertaking to homeschool one, two, or three children.

Unfortunately, the "homier than thou" attitude is growing within the homeschooling movement. We must do our best to squelch it in our own lives as individuals.

I am *not* saying that we should refrain from ever expressing an opinion on a controversial subject. If anyone wants to ask me why I am fully committed to courtship rather than dating, I will gladly and enthusiastically explain it. But I hope I do it in a way that is absent of pride and ultimately merciful.

I was recently reading the Book of James in my personal devotional time when a passage stood out to me for the first time. You know that one of the important themes of James is the concept that "faith without works is dead." James is really hard on people who try to believe the right things but live their lives in a manner different from their professed beliefs. James is a hard-core book. But in the midst of his book, James writes: "Speak and act as those who are going to be judged by the law that gives freedom, because judgment without mercy will be shown to anyone who has not been merciful. Mercy triumphs over judgment" (James 2:12–13).

The longer I walk with Christ, the tougher I try to be on myself. I do my best to hold myself to very high standards of excellence. However, the longer I walk with Christ, the more lenient I become on people who do things differently from the way I do them. I am glad to try to talk with such people and will often encourage them to see things my way, but I strive to be gracious. As homeschoolers, we need to be tough on ourselves and lenient with our fellow homeschoolers who have other distinctives.

Let me really go out on a limb. Even though I think that homeschooling is the greatest form of education, and that any parent can do a great job of homeschooling if they are willing to work hard, and even though I think that Scripture teaches me as a Christian father that this is my obligation to my children, I refuse to tell anyone else that it is a sin for them to fail to homeschool. There is only one Holy Spirit, and He "ain't" me. And He "ain't" you either.

We need to be gracious people to homeschoolers and to others as well. We need to "speak and act as those who are going to be judged by the law that gives freedom, because judgment without mercy will be shown to anyone who has not been merciful. Mercy triumphs over judgment."

Truly spiritual homeschoolers refrain from being "homier than thou." Let's be gracious people.

6

THANKS, MOM

Fall 1996

One of the special privileges I enjoy is the opportunity to interact with thousands of homeschooling parents every year at state homeschooling conferences and conventions. At every conference, people come up to me to express gratefulness and appreciation for the work of Home School Legal Defense Association. I am always specially moved by those who tell me that they pray for us on a regular basis. That means more to all of us at HSDLA than can ever be adequately explained.

But as I have been watching my wife, Vickie, begin the process of starting our family's fourteenth year in homeschooling, a question suddenly occurred to me: *Who thanks the real heroes of the homeschooling movement?*

Vickie is teaching five of our children who are of school age this year (two have graduated; two are too young). She is teaching a total of twenty-eight subjects. And she is washing and cooking and washing and cleaning and washing and driving and washing and shopping and washing and mending and washing—all on top of her teaching responsibilities.

Vickie is unusual compared to the world at large. And she is obviously uniquely special to me. But another two or three hundred thousand homeschooling moms are doing the same things.

And it's my guess that these ladies, the real heroes of the homeschooling movement, rarely hear words of thanks. So let me give it a try. Here is my letter to all homeschooling moms:

Thanks for being willing to sacrifice the minutes, hours, days, months, and years that constitute your life so that your children will have the opportunity to grow up godly, mature, wise, intelligent, and loving. People who give great sums of money are widely heralded as great philanthropists. You have given something of far greater value. You have given your children your very essence so that they may achieve the kind of greatness that God values. Keep in mind that their only hope for achieving those character qualities is bound up in the fact that you serve the one true God who endows you with those same characteristics.

Thank you for your plain old hard work. In the midst of a society bent on obtaining the maximum in convenience, you demonstrate that things of value are not accomplished quickly or on the first try. You are the exemplars of the virtue of the third, fourth, and fifth try. If your children take your example into the American workplace, our nation will rise to its former prominence as the country that succeeded because of its simple commitment to hard work.

Thank you for being willing to encourage other moms who struggle, who are new to the movement, who are discouraged,

who need your counsel, your experience, or your wisdom. Thanks also for the selflessness you demonstrate as you devote many hours so that other families may succeed. Arguably you have a vested interest in the success of your own children. You have nothing to gain from helping others. It is an act of pure altruism.

Thank you for your obedience to God. Together with your husband you have read the Scriptures. You have understood them to lead you in this path of home education. And regardless of the costs, the difficulties, or the lack of immediate rewards or gratification, you have done what is right simply because it is right. Few are willing to do right these days for its own sake. You serve as an example of moral courage that our leaders would do well to copy.

Thank you for loving your husband. Your marriage is the human foundation of your home. When it cracks and crumbles, all that you value, including your homeschooling, is threatened. Your selfless love for your husband is an essential ingredient to keeping that foundation strong and true.

Thank you for taking the time to teach your children the truth. So much of education today ignores the truth and simply attempts to impart knowledge separated from the principles of absolute truth that flow from Almighty God. Your children have the advantage of learning what is real and true and good. Those things that are cheap counterfeits will always be self-evident frauds to those who have had the good fortune to spend years being exposed to the truth.

And finally, thank you for being willing to swim against the stream of society's definition of success. Stay-at-home moms are vilified with faint praise in our society today. The "mothers of the year" are normally those who are "great moms," but they are really chosen because they also serve as captains of industry, public policy, or finance. At the very time the world ridicules a mom who devotes herself exclusively to her family, you have embraced that role with even more enthusiasm than the generations that have gone before you. Your version of "having it all" means shouldering all the responsibility for the rearing of your children.

The feminists won't hold a women's conference in China, or anywhere else, to give you the accolades you so richly deserve.

But your true reward will never be meager efforts of thanks like this letter. Your true reward, at least the one you will see here on earth, will be children who rise up while the rest of the world is stooping in compromise. Your children will rise up and call you blessed with their lives, their words, and their deeds. It is your legacy of love.

Thanks.

7

ADVANTAGES OF OLDER KIDS TEACHING YOUNGER KIDS

Fall 1998

At the Farris home this year we have six of our ten children who are now of school age, a record for us. Three have graduated from high school. Peter is only eighteen months old. That leaves us with kids in kindergarten, first, fifth, sixth, and ninth grades.

How does my wife, Vickie, teach six grades simultaneously? Good organization is part of the answer. Long days are another part of the answer. But our twenty-year-old daughter, Jayme, is also part of the answer.

Jayme graduated from high school as a National Merit Commended Scholar when she was fifteen. She was apprenticed as a graphic artist and editor for four years. She then spent 1997 in Romania working for a Christian college and in an orphanage organized by a remarkable young woman associated with the college.

Jayme now has two tasks on her immediate agenda. First, she has established her own nonprofit organization, Regeneration Ministries (P. O. 2027, Purcellville, VA 20134), to assist indigenous leaders of Christian organizations that help children in developing nations. Her initial major project is to raise the money for a new building for the Hope House Orphanage in Oradea, Romania. It's a worthwhile project that all segments of society can appreciate.

However, her second major agenda item is something that some elements of our politically correct society would question. Every morning Jayme is homeschooling her four- and six-year-old brothers. Her assistance to our family in this way is invaluable, especially in my wife's estimation. But it is also good for Jayme's future.

Jayme wants to accomplish many things in life that are far above average expectations for twenty-year-olds. But ultimately she wants to be a homeschooling mom raising her own family. Her season of instructing her younger brothers is ideal preparation for that task.

Not every homeschooling child will have the same focus as Jayme. But every homeschooling student can benefit from a season of preparation that comes from helping teach a younger child. And a student need not be seventeen or eighteen years old before he or she is able to help out.

When I was in the fifth grade, just after the Ice Age, three or four of us who were the best readers in our class were assigned to assist some of our classmates who were struggling with their reading. I hope it helped our classmates. I know it helped me develop patience and understanding of others. Both character qualities and reading were being taught simultaneously.

Older homeschool students can give their younger siblings a spelling test, drill math facts with flash cards, organize art projects, or teach a particular skill like calligraphy. One of our older daughters, Katie, is especially adept at sports and in the past she organized games and activities for her younger siblings that matched her interests.

At least three positive results are achieved when older homeschool kids help the younger. Younger students get needed academic assistance. Overworked homeschooling moms get reinforcements. And the creativity and character of the older student is stimulated in ways that pay long-term dividends.

It probably won't surprise anyone that Jayme was a great help to her younger brothers and sisters when she was in her early teens. Character with the vision and persistence to build an orphanage half a world away does not appear suddenly. It is the result of years of training and service.

When kids are isolated in age-segregated herds in institutional schools where the operating assumptions are that they will be served and entertained, parents must struggle to develop a servant's heart in their children. But when a child grows up in a large homeschooling family, learning to serve others is inherent in the process.

Others may brag about the academic success of home education. But I believe the greatest advantage of home education is the character that comes from learning to serve the needs of others.

GOD WRITES OUR
CHILDREN'S STORIES

Summer 1996

I am writing a novel. Whether it will be published is a different story.* In any event, I am writing a novel.

I have had a lot of fun creating characters, good guys and bad guys, good lawyers and bad lawyers (I know some think the phrase "bad lawyers" is redundant), and manipulating the details of their lives. I had the major points of the plot all worked out before I began writing, but I've been making up many of the minor details as I've gone along.

When I was about halfway through, I realized that I had made a miscalculation on some dates. So I had to go back and

---

*Actually Broadman & Holman has now published three of my novels. The latest is *Forbid Them Not.*

move all the events in the entire novel to make everything occur seven days earlier.

At that point, something occurred to me about the nature of God that I want to share with you.

God directs the affairs of men. Applying that principle on an individual level, God directs both the big events and the little events of each of our lives. And God not only directs the events of each of our lives individually, He is able to intertwine all the details of every life on earth—like one huge novel with several billion characters—and keep everything in perfect order. God never has to say, "Oops, I need to go back and move all the events back seven days. I forgot something." It is humbling to understand how much smarter God is than any human, to compare his ability to flawlessly write real human history, when we have difficulty keeping ten characters straight in a work of fiction.

Let's apply this principle to our lives as homeschooling parents.

In a sense, the act of raising our children can be compared with writing a story for each of them. We try to provide them training and experience to make them fit to serve the Lord, their families, their churches, and their nation. We arrange thousands of details and hope it all works out in the end for our children's good.

I am sure that many of you have found, as Vickie and I have found, that we are not perfect planners for our children. Nor do we always execute even our best plans perfectly. If the well-being of our children were dependent on us alone, something would go awry, and we would find that we had to go back and undo parts of the story and start over again.

Raising a child is a complicated endeavor, much too complicated for any human to perform perfectly.

The good news is that your children have another parent. They have a Heavenly Father who is superintending all the details of their lives. God in His sovereignty allows us free choice, but He always maintains full authority over every detail. I am not smart enough to figure out how He does all that. But then again I am not smart enough to write two hundred pages of fiction without needing to rewind and fix the details to fit the plot.

I only hope that I am smart enough to realize who is really in charge and that I spend adequate time each day talking to the God of the universe, who loves my children and me and wants every detail in our lives to work out for our best and His glory.

THE DANGEROUS MYTH
OF THE PERFECT
HOMESCHOOL MOM

You've seen her before. Maybe not in real life, but you've seen her on the cover of *The Teaching Home* or some other homeschooling magazine. Her thirteen children are all wearing matching outfits. They all have perfect hair—the twelve girls' hair rather long with matching ribbons—the boy like a little groom atop a wedding cake. Their teeth are perfect. The house is perfect. In fact, their children's outfits not only match each other, they even match the wallpaper in the dining room. The dishes on the table gleam.

The husband sits at the head of the table with a Bible that is six inches thicker than any you've ever owned. He has a devoted and loving stare focused on his wife. His very countenance is calling her blessed without speaking a single word.

Then there is the mother herself. Slyly hidden behind one of the children, but you have no doubt that behind that smile and the hair drawn back with a white lace ribbon, matching the collar on her dark blue jumper, this is one accomplished woman.

Inside the magazine we read her story.

She has managed to teach all of her children the history of the Roman Empire, three variable Algebra problems, the periodic table of elements, ancient Hebrew, and sentence diagramming using nothing but Psalm 137 and a few Legos for manipulatives.

Her twelve-year-old makes $18,000 a year selling muffins door-to-door. He donates half to the senior center where he and his twelve sisters sing and play the harp, piano, violin, and oboe each Wednesday afternoon before they recite another twelve sections each in their weekly Awana program.

She never uses a textbook—only original editions of publications that are no less than 150 years old, most from ancient Greece. Her nine-year-old has qualified for the National Spelling Bee, but mom never needs to coach her because her fifteen-year-old sister was the national champion three years earlier.

This is the perfect homeschooling mom. And nearly all homeschooling moms are just like her. Except you.

I happen to have some inside information. These magazine covers use mannequins, and the stories of the families are written by aspiring novelists.

The perfect homeschooling mom is a myth created for the sole purpose of stealing your joy.

If the myth of the perfect homeschooling mom doesn't get you, the image of the perfect public school teacher will. She doesn't just teach; she enriches. She may be in the public school system, which by federal court order cannot mention God in a positive manner, but she is actually a fine Christian from your church who graduated from a top-notch Christian college. Her little character lessons are cleverly disguised Bible stories. Her class is orderly. Her children behave. Your child would be so much better off in her class *learning all those things he is supposed to know.*

When we reduce these mythological characters to their essential terms, what is this fear that captures so many homeschooling mothers? It is the fear that their child is missing out on something essential.

Is this fear realistic? How do you know if you are doing the right thing with your children? How can you be sure that you are not ruining their lives?

Let's look at some of the specific issues that arise when homeschooling moms start to worry that they are failing some aspect of the test of perfection.

Am I Homeschooling the Right Way?

If you have hung around homeschooling for any length of time you have heard this one: "We shouldn't be doing school at home. We should be homeschooling."

This slogan has become a pet peeve of mine. Frankly, I don't believe those who say this have any idea what they are talking about. My evidence? After a while, these same people will say, "There is no one right way to do homeschooling." Well, if this is true (and I think it is), then whatever it is that they call "school at home" is also subject to the rule that "there is no one right way to do homeschooling."

Some moms feel guilty that they are using textbooks, not "real books." Other moms say that they only know how to do curriculum that "comes out of a box."

In the event that some homeschooling "expert" gives a presentation that makes you feel guilty about the way you are homeschooling (or the way you would like to homeschool), let me give you a trump card. No matter what expertise the homeschooling expert claims to have, I can top them. (I only say this to convince you that they have no right to belittle the way you are homeschooling.) *Education Week* is the biggest education news publication in the nation. It listed me as one of the Top 100 Faces in Education for the Twentieth Century, the only homeschool leader listed. That gives me some sort of "authority."

So here is my trump card of authority just for you: "You should homeschool with whatever curriculum you like. As long as it is adequate to teach the basics (more on this later), it doesn't have to be perfect. The number-one factor in curriculum selection is this: Is this easy for you to use? If it isn't easy on mom, don't buy it."

OK. I hear you. You appreciate my trump card, but you would like something more substantial, some rationale supporting my position.

Most Christians recognize that their ultimate reasons for homeschooling are spiritual. This does not mean you do not want your children to do well academically, but in balancing the priorities, you believe that spiritual matters come first.

The core spiritual goal is to transmit your faith from one generation to the next. Teaching our children to love God is more important than teaching them to diagram sentences. And we know that God endorses the method of spending time with your children as the best means of teaching your children to love God (see Deuteronomy 6 for details).

You cannot do everything. It is not a mere matter of being better organized. You simply cannot do everything. There are never twenty-nine hours in a day, and even that would be inadequate to do everything.

There are hundreds of interesting ideas that you could present to your children. There are thousands of wonderful books. But which of these many choices is the best is simply a matter of opinion. The truth is that there are more good choices than you will ever have time to pursue.

So you have to decide which area of your life is going to get less than the very best you can give. You cannot be the greatest homeschooling mom, the greatest wife, the greatest women's Bible study leader, the greatest church pianist, the greatest neighborhood evangelist, the greatest cook, the greatest housekeeper, and the greatest wife that ever existed all at the same time.

You need to decide which areas are the most important and devote more of your resources and your incredibly precious time to those projects. You must let lesser priorities slide, either a little or a lot.

Being a mother is a high priority, but it must not be your highest priority. You need to give a higher priority to your husband.

This does not mean that you will spend more time taking care of your husband in the course of the day than you spend with your children. It does mean that you cut a few corners with your kids so that you have a little emotional reserve left at night to be with your husband. If this means teaching curriculum that comes from a box rather than the nifty "real books" curriculum you would love to design, then use the box and yield yourself a little more time with your husband.

If your curriculum choices leave you no time to study the Word so that you have spiritual sustenance not only for yourself but to pass along to your children, then get a curriculum that is easier to use.

If your homeschool support group activities are wonderfully enriching but steal time you need to transmit your values to your children, don't go.

Your children need a sane mother far more than they need a support group. (Maybe you want to adapt this sentence to your own situation and tape it over your kitchen sink as a reminder.)

As president of the college most closely associated with the homeschooling movement—a college with a deserved reputation for attracting the academic elite of the movement—I can tell you that there are plenty of students at Patrick Henry College whose mothers got their curriculum out of a box. Many did "school at home." Few taught their children Latin or Greek during their high school years. And I have never seen a family during orientation week all wearing matching clothes.

Academic success goes hand in hand with the personal sanity of the teaching parent. Successful moms are happy moms who have established real priorities for themselves and their children.

Am I Covering the True Academic Priorities?

In light of what I have just said, my answer to this question is going to be a matter of opinion. In this case, it will be my opinion. You are completely free to find other opinions, and that will be just fine. But my opinion is pretty consistent with my "keep mom sane" philosophy of home education.

Children need to master only two areas of education, though they should be exposed to a great variety of other aspects of education.

The first area that I believe should be mastered is the English language. This includes reading, spelling, grammar, and writing. This is sometimes called Language Arts. One cannot truly learn any other subject without first mastering the ability to read and write.

There is no doubt that the vast majority of children should learn to read through the method of intensive phonics. After all, in English letters make sounds. Children should be taught to decode those sounds.

Moreover, they should be taught to write well. Spelling and grammar are the building blocks of great writing. We have found the A Beka grammar books to be outstanding in drilling the basics into our children.

It is not enough to know the rules of grammar and to memorize spelling words. Children should actually learn to write something. The best instruction I ever received in writing was this: "Read a lot of good writing. Write a lot." I personally think that my own writing improved dramatically after I read C. S. Lewis's Chronicles of Narnia aloud to my children several times. Lewis writes clear prose that sings.

While on the point of reading aloud, I learned from being an editor on the *Gonzaga Law Review* that reading aloud is the best way to proofread. I recommend this to my students at Patrick Henry. Reading a paper aloud is by far the most productive way to catch the errors that their eyes would otherwise skim past.

By the time you have finished homeschooling your children, they should be masters of the language. This, to me, is essential.

The other subject that needs to be mastered is mathematics. Math is the language for the world of science, but it also impacts business and many other fields.

This is one area where homeschool students do not consistently outperform public school students. Homeschool kids do very well in the early stages of math, but by the time our students get into the upper grades, they are only slightly ahead of public school students in math.

Although I do not believe that every student needs to take Calculus, getting through Algebra I and II and Geometry is pretty basic.

You may find it necessary to get outside help with math. Sometimes dad can take over for mom in the higher levels of math. (In the Farris home, Vickie is better at higher math, and I prefer to teach literature, contrary to all the stereotypes.) Sometimes students can enroll in a local community college for some of these upper division courses. It is becoming increasingly possible to take some upper division math courses online. Patrick Henry College launched an online College Algebra class in September 2002. There are other choices as well.

Math and language arts are the only two subjects that need to be *mastered* while your children are being homeschooled. This does not mean that these are all your kids study. But they may be the only subjects that are in your curriculum every single year.

Everything else falls into the category of exposure. I think your children should be exposed to history, literature, science, art, music, and physical education.

Obviously, some of these subjects are *very* important. But your children will not master all these subjects before graduating from high school. Language and math are the tools for learning, and the tools should be mastered. History, literature, science, art, music, and physical education are the substance of learning. One can devote a lifetime to any one of these fields without truly mastering it.

This important distinction between mastery and exposure can help you keep your sanity. If you think that your children should reach a true mastery of history and science, for example, you will fail. However, if you think that they should get a good, in-depth exposure to these topics so that they are generally familiar with them, then you can succeed.

I believe that storytelling makes these subjects come alive. A student who has learned an interesting story on some facet of a subject is far more likely to be willing to vigorously undertake the general subject.

For example, a student who has read *A Tale of Two Cities* or *The Scarlet Pimpernel* (two of my all-time favorite novels) is much more likely to be interested in studying the French Revolution.

Someone who reads the great new biography *John Adams* by David McCullough is much more likely to want to understand and study the period of the Founding Fathers. (This particular book is the best I've ever read for understanding why it was so important to change from the Articles of Confederation to the Constitution).

At the younger ages, *Why America Is Free* is the best book I have discovered for telling the basic story of American history from 1750 to 1800, which is clearly the most crucial period. It tells the story in an interesting format, in a way that appeals to children and even adults.

Another favorite of mine is the book *Wide as the Waters* by Benson Bobrick. This is the incredible story of Wycliffe, Tyndale,

61

and the other courageous men who translated the English Bible and got it into the hands of the common people. Although this book is by a secular author and publisher, its conclusion is that without getting the English Bible into the hands of the common people, self-government would never have been possible in the United States, and the free world as we know it would not exist.

Reading *Wide as the Waters* will teach readers more about the English monarchy than any amount of drilling to memorize names and dates. It becomes a lot easier to undertake a more general study of English history afterwards because the student will have an underlying story line already in mind when he begins.

Biographies are particularly helpful in exposing your children to history. In the younger grades, reading biographies may be all that is needed to begin your efforts to expose your children to history.

Sometime in grades five through twelve, your child should get a broad exposure to history, science, literature, art, and music. Some of these subjects need to be in your exposure category every year. But your child does not need to finish every page of every book that you have purchased. You are seeking broad exposure, with flashes of in-depth learning that come when your child is truly fascinated by a subject. Most of these in-depth experiences must await the upper levels. Mom needs only to open the door and let her child charge ahead.

One goal of education is to prepare our children for citizenship. Although your students will not master the Constitution, they should be exposed to it, especially during their high school years.

When our two oldest daughters reached high school, I couldn't find a book on constitutional law that seemed appropriate, so I wrote one myself. To save you the trouble of having to do that yourself, I have published *Constitutional Law for Christian Students*. This book is available (together with a CD-ROM and an online course) through Home School Legal Defense Association (www.hslda.org). But even with constitutional law (my favorite subject) the goal is exposure, not mastery.

I hope you find the distinction between exposure and mastery liberating for you as a homeschooling mom. It would be sad for me if this idea were twisted in a way that would discourage a student from trying to become excellent. There are very few mothers who willingly give up on the idea of excellence for their children. My goal in this section has been to bring some balance and sanity into our notions of what constitutes excellence. If you think you have to master it all, you will not make it, and both you and your children will become frustrated.

Master the true basics (language and math), get a well-rounded exposure in the other areas, and your children will turn out just fine.

Am I a Failure If My House Doesn't Look Like Martha Stewart's?

Vickie has already confessed the basics in her book *A Mom Just like Me*. Our house is not spotless when I walk in the door from work. There are dishes in the sink (or on the table) on many school days. Wash that needs to be folded gets stacked up. The floor may well need sweeping. And you can find stray toys in just about any room of the house at that hour of the day. But by the time we go to bed, the dishes are always done, and our home looks straightened up. You could find dust on some furniture and crumbs in some corners. Our home is basically neat and clean, but it does not look anything like those pictures you see in a home decorating magazine.

Few homeschoolers' homes look anything like these magazine pictures. But many moms are paralyzed by guilt anyway.

At HSLDA we deal with a number of serious social worker investigation cases each year. Some portion of these include the allegation of a messy home. In a few cases, the allegation has at least some merit. But these are less than five homes per year out of over seventy thousand member families.

If you have any of these kinds of issues on a regular basis, then you may have a problem:

- Garbage (including dirty diapers) collecting in the interior of the home
- Dishes that have not been done for several days
- Food scraps left out for days at a time where bugs and mold are present
- Bathrooms that haven't been cleaned in weeks
- Bedding that hasn't been changed in several weeks
- Constant (not occasional) clutter that interferes with normal operations of life

Most of you are recoiling in horror at the thought of such things in your home. Good. You are normal.

Every normal home has occasional unmade beds, unwashed dishes, toys on the floor, and clothes on the bedroom floor.

If your home looks decent sometime in the day on most days, then do not sweat the details. If it looks decent only once a month, then you may want to pick up the pace a bit.

Thus far I have been talking about these issues with only your mental well-being in mind. There are two other relevant sorts of people in your home that need to be considered.

One is your children. They are your workers. You are the manager. Make them help you clean the home as soon as they are old enough to do so. Certainly by the time they are five or six, they can become a real asset in this process.

Vickie was an only child. I was one of four children, but my mom was one of eleven. Vickie's mom did most of the housework while Vickie was at school, and so Vickie concentrated on her studies. She had little experience in many aspects of housekeeping when we got married.

Not only was my mom quite willing to have us help out for our own good, she needed help because she had serious health problems—five back surgeries and, later on, multiple sclerosis. This required us children to carry more of the load.

Because of her own childhood, Vickie feels more guilt about our children's workload in one week than has ever crossed my mind in a lifetime. She agrees with me in her head, but her emotions at times tell her that the kids need to play more. (They have many hours each day for free time and play.)

Here is my motto: They eat the food and help make the mess, and they can help keep it clean.

While your husband should help with household matters as well, he will have to read my book *The Homeschooling Father* to get beat over the head with that lesson. For now, I am talking to moms. Sure you would like (and deserve) his help, but let's look at other aspects of your husband's views on housekeeping and how they affect the relatively laid-back advice I have already offered.

Let me give it to you straight: your husband's standards, not mine, should prevail in your home.

If you want to show him what I have written to get him to consider other ways of thinking, fine. But don't be surprised when he points to this section where I say, ultimately, he should set the standards for the home after you have asked him to thoughtfully consider all alternatives.

Few husbands want to control the details here. Most are big-picture thinkers when considering housekeeping. If things are usually good, then an occasional variation won't cause a major issue for most men.

However, some men feel a need for more order and cleanliness than I have outlined. If that is your husband's case, then I would encourage you to have a serious conversation with your husband about the level of responsibility you are carrying. (I am constantly surprised at the number of men and women who don't try to communicate about their needs and expectations in marriage.) Don't whine. Don't gripe. Don't threaten. Simply explain the duties you have, and tell your husband that you don't find it possible to get everything done that needs to get done and that you need his help in setting proper priorities. Some things will have to slide from time to time. Let him tell you what should slide when he has communicated expectations that you don't think you can meet. A cry for help should engender a reasonable response from your husband. An explosion of bitter feelings will only backfire.

Most women worry about household order more than their husbands do. If you are driving yourself crazy worrying about an immaculate home, please give yourself a break and recognize that the perfect homeschool mom doesn't exist and that you don't have to be the first one.

What If My Children Misbehave?

There is a hidden danger in answering questions like this in writing. The danger is giving a one-size-fits-all answer. Some moms need to hear the message, "Lighten up with your kids. You are being a bit overzealous." Others need to hear, "It might be a good idea to be a bit more consistent in disciplining your children."

I once did a homeschool case that illustrates the problem with one-size-fits-all teaching on child rearing.

The case involved a young homeschool teen who committed a serious crime against another homeschool student. Because of his crime, the authorities wanted to remove his family's ability to homeschool any of their children.

This family was following a homeschool program that emphasized strict discipline and strong lines of authority.

The local attorney that we hired was also a homeschooling dad whose family was enrolled in this same very structured homeschool program.

The attorney's home reminded me of my own family. There was a lot of fun and laughter and a little bit of chaos. I know that my family could occasionally use a good dose of the message of that we should be a bit more consistent.

The family that was taken to court was just the opposite. Both mom and dad were very naturally oriented toward a strict sense of orderliness and instant obedience.

Although I believed that the young man who had done wrong was fully responsible for his own wrongful behavior, my impression at the time was that he had been susceptible to weakness in part because of the stress that I observed in his family. The message that family needed to hear was to lighten up once in a while.

I trust that you will prayerfully ask yourself on which side of this continuum your family falls. Some of you need to be more careful to discipline. Some need to be more willing to be merciful.

A wife alone or a husband alone will have blind spots on this, so please talk with each other and see if you can agree on your family's natural strengths and weaknesses.

Having said all this, let me address the mother who is worried about her children being perfect. Here's a good rule of thumb to check, whether you are overreacting or you actually should tighten your discipline. Has anyone ever come up to you in public and said, "My, you have wonderful children! They are so well-behaved!"

If that has happened to you several times and you are still worried about having perfect children, then you are the mom I want to talk to.

Your children need to be well behaved, but they cannot be perfect. The Bible says so: "All have sinned and fall short of the glory of God" (Romans 3:23). You can and should punish them for deliberate misbehavior. But if you are excessively worried about this, your concern is not the well-being of your children but the embarrassment you suffer when your child publicly exhibits human sinfulness. You may have to dig deep to see what your true motivation is. It is easy to deceive oneself in this situation.

Everyone else in the world is judging your children by their frame of reference, which is comparing them to their own children and other children they know. Very few children are their very best at home. Almost all moms and dads see the lowest level of behavior exhibited by their children.

When your children act inappropriately in front of another family, you are thinking, *I have never seen the Smith children behave this badly.* Maybe you haven't, but I can guarantee you that the Smiths have seen their children act this badly and even worse at home.

The principle that can liberate you from a whole lot of worrisome comparisons is this: Deal with your children according to what they have done. Don't let your fear of the reactions of other people cause you to deviate from punishment if deserved, or mercy if warranted.

I remember one time we were talking with one of our older daughters about a bad attitude. She said something like, "Well, at least I am not taking drugs or sleeping with boys like most girls my age." She may have had a bad attitude, but she was right. At that moment, I appreciated her comment, though at other times it might have made me mad. We sometimes need perspective. If we demand perfection of ourselves in our child rearing, we will be disappointed. If we demand perfect behavior from our children, they will never achieve it. Standing for what is right while administering discipline with love and mercy is a tricky balance, one that is too hard for parents unassisted. God alone can give you the wisdom to know which way to turn in situations that require so much finesse and a quick understanding of the truth.

10

END-OF-THE-YEAR BLUES

Ready for school to be over for the year? I mean, are you really ready for June? Isn't it hard to wait? If so, you must be the mom in a homeschooling family.

While a few irresponsible homeschool promoters try to convince parents that this is easy, most seasoned veterans tell a more realistic story. Homeschooling is a lot of hard work. And if you have to live someplace like Virginia, where the spring blossoms and sun and green grass are yelling your name at about 2:00 in the afternoon, you just don't feel like finishing another two hours of work.

So what do you do?

The short answer is that you behave like an adult. An adult looks past a spring afternoon and sees the long-range benefit of a child's education. An adult gets up when the alarm goes off in the morning rather than sleeping until noon. An adult does what it takes to accomplish that which is important.

Children break off relationships for petty reasons. Children live for the moment. Children do the fun thing first and the important thing later, if they get around to it. Children forget to do their assignments. Children blame others when things go wrong.

The sad reality is that the world beckons and encourages adults to behave like children. The world entices us with easy divorce instead working hard to preserve our marriages. The world says live for today, not for tomorrow and certainly not for ten years from tomorrow. The world says that the fault for our failures lies with society, or our upbringing, or San Andreas.

Bill Clinton's personal life exemplifies the call of the child. A homeschool mom who completes the year when she would rather take a break demonstrates what being an adult is all about.

The blessing of being an adult is having an adult's perspective on rewards. A child needs instant gratification. An adult can wait.

Sending your child back to the public schools next year provides instant relief from the hard work. But the homeschool mom who perseveres year after year, and especially spring after spring, will someday see her child grow up with solid academics, socialization, and spiritual maturity. A child who grows straight and true is clearly more important than anything offered by the moment. The big prizes take a long time to win.

Homeschool moms do an adult's work and receive an adult's reward.

GOD USES TEMPORAL NEEDS TO ACHIEVE SPIRITUAL RESULTS

In Acts 6 we read about the appointment of the first deacons in the early church in Jerusalem. The apostles appointed deacons because of a dispute between the Hebraic and Greek widows concerning the distribution of food. The apostles said, "It would not be right for us to neglect the ministry of the word of God in order to wait on tables" (Acts 6:2).

Have you ever noticed the unusual qualifications the apostles employed in selecting people for "waiting on tables"? They directed the congregation to choose men "who are known to be full of the Spirit and wisdom."

But apparently their method worked. We hear nothing more about this dispute over food. Instead, we are told that the church experienced even greater growth and that even some Jewish priests converted to the faith.

The clear lesson from this episode is that meeting temporal needs is one of the methods God uses to achieve spiritual results. And in order to make this happen, we need to be highly concerned about the spiritual qualifications of those whom we select to meet temporal needs.

Notice also that even though the apostles did not have the time to wait on tables themselves, they had the time to participate in selecting and dedicating these deacons. And they had the time to pray for them. Their time was supposed to be devoted to spiritual matters. Developing other leaders was among the tasks that constituted the highest and best use of their time.

How does this apply to homeschooling parents?

We are busy people, as busy as any group of people in America. At times we are stretched so thin that we simply do not have the time to meet all the temporal needs we encounter. We need not feel guilty about this. Instead, when we encounter needs we are unable to meet, we should look for opportunities to develop other leaders who will be able to move into the gap.

This has an obvious application for those who lead state and local homeschool associations and support groups. Developing additional leaders is one of the highest and best uses of your time.

But all homeschooling families should consider our children as leaders in the making. When we cannot "wait on tables," we should be working for the day when our children can.

The academic instruction we provide our children is one way in which we prepare our children for future service and leadership. But it is far from the most important way. Our ultimate goal for our children should be to raise young men and women who are "known to be full of the Spirit and wisdom." When such young people are placed in the path of people with temporal needs, there will often be a spiritual harvest.

When I was running for lieutenant governor of Virginia a few years ago, I had an eighteen-year-old homeschool graduate who was one of my drivers. He was with me one night as I participated in a "town hall" styled meeting on Outcome-Based Education, which was a hot political issue that year. The meeting was held in a church but was not a church-related function in any way.

This young man had two tasks that evening: to drive me and to put out literature. He didn't need to be spiritually qualified to do either of those tasks, but he was.

A man wandered in off the street after the meeting had begun. He asked my driver what the meeting was about. He was told that it concerned Outcome-Based Education. The man had no interest in the topic but expressed a spiritual need that had drawn him into a church that evening. My driver talked with this man and a little while later led him through a prayer to accept Jesus Christ as his personal Savior.

If we had selected a driver based solely on the ability to drive and pass out literature, we would have missed the opportunity to help a person with the most important issue of his life. Because this young man's parents and church had prepared him for spiritual maturity, his temporal service gave him an opportunity to meet spiritual needs.

Incidentally, this young man, Rich Shipe, is now my son-in-law, married to my oldest daughter, Christy.

When we train our children to know and love God deeply, and to have the humble hearts to wait tables, drive candidates, or mow lawns, there is every reason to believe that we will reap spiritual rewards that far exceed our human expectations.

SUMMER SCHOOL

I recently spoke at a conference for law students just outside of Fraser, Colorado. Just out the back door of the main lodge there was a small trout pond that yelled my name whenever I had a free moment. The salmon eggs I got from the store didn't seem to work too well. But when I turned over a good-sized rock, I got a few small worms that produced a few nibbles from the elusive trout.

Fishing in the Rocky Mountains was extremely nostalgic for me (despite the general view that nostalgia isn't quite what it used to be). My family spent several summer weeks in that part of Colorado during my childhood. I did a lot of fishing with a willow branch, a bit of fishing line, a hook, and a couple sinkers.

It seemed to me that there are some old-fashioned pleasures of childhood summers that our kids don't seem to know these days. So I propose to my fellow homeschoolers and parents in general that we adopt a summer curriculum that consists of teaching our kids some things that used to be the sine qua non of summers and childhood.

Here are a few of my suggested courses for parent-taught summer school.

Teach your kids to fish. Learning how to bait a hook may help develop the skills that could develop a future surgeon. Figuring out how to untangle a snarled line is the equivalent of a three-credit course in law school.

Go out in the backyard at night, sit down in the grass, and teach your kids to identify and name some of the basic constellations.

Get a pocketknife and teach your kids how to whittle. Some can make small figures of animals. My specialty as a child was your basic pointed stick.

Teach your children how to play hopscotch. You need some chalk, a small object for a marker, and pretty good knees to absorb all the jumping.

For heaven's sake, teach your kids to swim. This is not only fun; it's basic safety.

If you don't know how to play Steal the Flag, ask around your office until you find someone who knows. Go outside at night and play it with your kids and the kids in the neighborhood. If your running skills aren't what they used to be, be the jail guard.

Plan a garden with your children. The world has a major zucchini shortage, and you can help solve this crisis.

Find a farm that allows you to pick your own strawberries. If you have a choice between taking your child to the top of the Eiffel Tower or to a field of strawberries, I think your better choice is to go get a few quarts of sweet, ripe fruit off the vine.

Teach your children to play jacks. It was supposedly a girls' game when I was a kid, but my older sister was trying to be a state jacks champion, and she taught me the game to have some practice. If it hadn't been for blatant gender discrimination, I could have been a contender. And I hereby challenge any member of the national staff of the National Organization for Women to a game of jacks. Name the stakes, and I will smoke you.

OK, marbles also. I wasn't nearly as good at this one.

Go for a hike. Teach your kids the names of trees and flowers as you go along. Also, teach them the fine art of selecting an appropriate hiking stick.

Perhaps best of all, teach them how to read a book by flashlight while being crammed down inside of a sleeping bag.

Have a great summer.

ETERNAL PERSPECTIVE MAKES PRIORITIES CLEARER

I was writing my column. I was trying to address a number of disputes that have arisen among homeschoolers. The old dispute between Christian and non-Christian homeschoolers has erupted publicly, mostly through secular sources. And in the middle of writing, my secretary walked in and handed me the following letter.

Dear HSLDA staff,

On Good Friday, March 29, in the early hours of the morning, God took our oldest son, Jim, home to be with Him.

Jim had flown to California with his fourteen-year-old cousin on March 26 to visit my parents for twelve days. They had gone to Disneyland Thursday

and were having a great time when Jim got off a ride
and complained of back pain and started vomiting.

My parents took Jim to Scripps Hospital for
X rays. They were there a couple of hours before doc-
tors realized that Jim was "extraordinarily ill"; that he
was bleeding to death of a torn aorta.

A heart surgical team was assembled quickly, and
they began an echocardiogram, where they could see
the tear. They were going to do an angiogram when
Jim collapsed. They took him immediately into sur-
gery, but there was nothing they could do. The aorta
wasn't just torn; it was shredded. God took Jim to be
with Him three days before Jim's fourteenth birthday.

We are now awaiting the autopsy report to find
out what caused the aorta to be so weak. Scripps
Hospital and the San Diego County medical examiner
have said they had never seen this happen to such a
young boy. But we know that God makes no mistakes.

Jim had been surrounded with Christian nurses at
the hospital. My mom and dad were allowed to stay in
the room with Jim. My parents had prayed with him,
along with one of the nurses, even before they knew
how serious Jim's condition was. My mom says that
right after the prayer Jim's eyes and face just glowed
and a peace and calm came over him, which never left
him. God was with Jim every step of the way.

How thankful we are that we have homeschooled
Jim and our other two boys for the last six years! We
have seen Jim grow and mature in a way most parents
never experience. We were able to spend many hours

a day with him. We have so many keepsakes and memories.

My brother-in-law, who had gone on many of the Disneyland rides with Jim, said, "Jim had an innocence about him. You could tell that he was untouched by the world."

We cannot see the "whole picture." But God can. God will use this for good because He promised! Already we are amazed to hear of so many lives that have been touched by Jim's home-going—lives that may never have been touched otherwise. Praise the Lord!

We miss Jim so! We love him so! It hurts to have him away from us, but at the same time we have a peace and assurance that comes from God. He is our Rock and our Shield. We put our trust in Him.

Sincerely,

(Names withheld)

I just couldn't go on. The tears were overwhelming.

God used their letter to graciously give me His perspective on the whole matter. Through this letter I understood that God does not want us to waste *any* time on petty disputes and gossip. There are real people who are accomplishing mighty things for God in the lives of their children who need our help.

So let others rage in vain. Let the rest of us ignore these disputings, bickerings, and gossip and keep our eyes on the goal of helping families who want to raise a godly seed.

We have precious children whom the Lord has entrusted to us. We have been given a high calling. Let's use the days and hours we have to make a difference in the lives of children. Anything less constitutes a waste of the time the Lord has given us. You never know when your time is going to run out.

An eternal perspective has a way of making your priorities a whole lot clearer.

THE DANGERS OF PLAYING WITH ROMANCE

Spring 1998

Last Saturday a fourteen-year-old boy lay brain dead in a Mississippi hospital waiting only for his organs to be removed for transplants. The cause of his death was a self-inflicted gunshot wound. The cause of his despair was a romantic breakup with his girlfriend.

In the initial news reports of the tragedy in Jonesboro, Arkansas, where four students and a teacher were murdered outside Westside Middle School, it was widely reported that thirteen-year-old Mitch Johnson acted in revenge for a romantic breakup with a twelve-year-old girl.

The public soul searching that has followed in the wake of Jonesboro has been dominated by discussions of the danger of children playing with guns. Not one voice has been raised highlighting the danger of children playing with romance. The Mississippi boy who took his own life and the Arkansas boy who took the lives of others were both playing an emotional game that is simply inappropriate for children of these ages.

Among homeschooling families there is wide agreement that one of the greatest advantages of our educational methodology is that it removes our children from the pressures and dangers of immature dating. Homeschoolers have trained their children in courtship, which takes a tack for romance completely different from the practices that dominate our culture.

Under the philosophy of courtship, all romantic relationships are reserved until the season of life when a person is ready to be married. And there is a strong view that a young man is not ready to be married until he is ready to support a family. That normally delays any kind of pairing off until the early twenties for young men and the late teens for young women.

The second major operating principle of courtship is that there is no such thing as casual dating. Any date is undertaken with a mutual understanding between both of the young people and their parents that these young people are checking each other out with a serious belief that their relationship *may* lead to marriage.

Profamily conservatives have long preached that young people should abstain from sexual intercourse before marriage. Liberals have scoffed at such advice as unrealistic platitudes. Homeschoolers who have bought into the idea of courtship believe the liberals have a point. Sexual abstinence is extraordinarily difficult when a teenager has been pursuing emotional romance since age twelve and a physical relationship that stops short of intercourse for about the same length of time. It is unrealistic to expect that kids who have been "falling in love" since age twelve and been "messing around" since age thirteen will remain virgins until they marry a decade or so later.

The solution is not found in issuing condoms in elementary schools and birth control pills in middle schools. Rather, parents need to understand that their young teenagers are simply too young to handle either the physical or emotional side of a romantic relationship.

Sexually transmitted diseases, unwanted pregnancies, depression, academic decline, suicide, and murder are among the progeny of premature romance. When love and marriage are linked, these problems are substantially reduced or eliminated.

Two of my grown daughters will get married this year to the only boyfriends they have ever had. They have known dozens of guys because we encouraged all kinds of group activities where there has been a mixture of both sexes. Courtship has dominated their group activities, and pairing off has been off-limits unless the couple is ready to declare themselves ready for marriage and headed on that path with each other.

Every bride and groom say to each other, at least implicitly, that they "love each other with all their heart." For those who have dated, in reality they can only say that they love their intended with the shreds of their heart that remain. Little pieces of one's heart are given away each time a romance of any magnitude has blossomed. But when my oldest daughter, Christy, and Rich walk the aisle in August, their promise to love with all their hearts will be literally true since neither has ever had another love.

I know the idea sounds radical to a culture addicted to premature and illicit sex. But aren't Jonesboro and the sad experience of the young boy in Mississippi enough of an impetus for all of us to think a little differently?

SELF-ESTEEM AND ACHIEVEMENT

Bill Bennett was the first person who widely broadcast the disturbing fact that there is a wide disparity between public school student achievement and student self-esteem. American students rank number one in the world in self-esteem about their math skills and dead last among industrialized nations in actual math performance.

A recent study published in the *American School Board Journal* demonstrates that public school students come by their invalid conceits honestly. The *Journal* published the results of a survey of public school administrators that asked them to compare the effectiveness of home education with that of public education. Guess what? Public school administrators had very high self-esteem for their schools and a very low opinion of home education.

We wouldn't waste a dime of HSLDA money to commission a survey of homeschoolers to ask them to do a comparison of our form of education with public schools. What should we expect? Homeschoolers think we're better.

Next let's survey Hertz employees and ask them if they think Hertz or Avis is a better car rental company. Come on!

The answers to most of the questions posed by the *Journal* survey can be objectively ascertained. For example, 34 percent of the public school administrators said that homeschoolers were required to be tested in their state while 56 percent said that no testing was required. Why didn't the pollsters from Xavier University just look at the legal requirements of each state and find out the answer to that question?

By the way, testing (or an alternative form of review) is required in 60 percent of the states and not required in 40 percent of the states. All that the survey proves is that the school administrators are not actually familiar with the law in their states (or that the "researchers" didn't know how to pick a representative sample).

School administrators do not have a very high opinion of the academic success of homeschools versus public schools. Fifty-five percent of public school administrators believe that homeschoolers do not meet the academic standards set by their state. Sixty-three percent say that "homeschoolers don't make the grade," whatever that is supposed to mean. And not a single administrator in the nation said that students benefit more from instruction at home than in the classroom. Only 1 percent of the public school administrators said that homeschoolers do better on standardized achievement tests than public school students.

Dozens of studies (as distinguished from opinion polls) demonstrate that homeschool students score between 20 and

30 percentile points higher than their public school counterparts on standardized achievement tests.

Which is more reliable? A straight comparison of actual test results? Or a one-sided opinion poll of public school leaders?

It is fair to conclude that 99 percent of the leaders of the cult of self-esteem are objectively wrong when it comes to their belief about the results of comparative testing between homeschoolers and public schoolers.

This would all be the subject for a big laugh on how silly so-called research has become except that in every state of the country, this highly partisan, misinformed group of administrators has been given certain amounts of legal authority to enforce the laws that govern homeschoolers. This is the same as giving Hertz managers the ability to enforce the car rental laws against Avis. It is obvious from reading this survey that public school officials are engaging in the practice pyschologists describe as denial. People who have their egos on the line should not be given the power to enforce the laws against those who tend to diminish their self-esteem.

Homeschoolers need to realize that we have a long way to go in our battle to be free from unwarranted legal harrassment. In addition to the legal battles we wage here, one of our best defenses is solid research that objectively shows our success.

I would encourage you to support, financially and otherwise, the National Home Education Research Institute headed by Dr. Brian Ray. It is an independent organization that does initial research and reviews and reports on the research of others on home education.

If you would like to support NHERI, its address is:

National Home Education Research Institute

P. O. Box 13939

Salem, OR 97309–1939

www.nheri.org

tel. 503–364–1490

You can be guaranteed that you will never see NHERI conduct an opinion poll of homeschool partisans and call it research.

THE CONSPIRACY AGAINST CHURCH AND DECENCY

Spring 2001

Vickie and I took our seven unmarried children to the mall nine days before Easter. It was our annual trek to search for new clothes for the occasion. The older our kids get, the more frustrating this has become.

Michael is twelve. We went to the two large department stores that anchor the mall. Neither store had anything other than $75 navy blue blazers that could arguably be called boys' "church clothes" unless your definition of "church clothes" is a T-shirt without pictures on the front. There were some really cute church clothes for our four-year-old son, but once you cross over from "toddler" size to "little boys" size, church clothes disappear from the racks.

The next night we went to an outlet mall. Michael and I went to every store in the entire hundred-plus store conglomeration to look for boys' church clothes. No place had anything at all—not even $75 blue blazers.

There is an old ethnic joke (which I have changed for our politically correct times since telling jokes concerning nations of Eastern European origin are insensitive): "How do you know the groom at a 'Blogdovian' wedding?" "He's the guy with the clean bowling shirt." A "clean T-shirt" variant of that joke is being played out on families all over America who would just like to buy their sons some church clothes. Not everyone can afford blue blazers. Even if you can, no boy wants to wear the blue blazer every week.

But as bad as the situation is with boys, girls' clothes are far, far worse.

We have daughters who are ten, fourteen, and sixteen. They are all relatively short, although our fourteen-year-old gives signs that someday she will wear normal-sized women's clothing rather than the petites her mother wears.

The first department store did not have a junior section, so our girls tried the petites and children's clothing sections. Frustration. Little girls' dresses that are decent (not all are) all look like someone dumped a quart of syrup and six yards of lace on top of a white pinafore. Sickly sweet. Even I didn't like any of them. Many dresses would have had potential had they not had a white, crumpled flower the size of the national debt sewn right in the middle of the bust. More importantly, fourteen-year-old girls don't want to look like five-year-old girls.

The petite women's section just looked too old on our sixteen-year-old. Not risqué old. Matronly old.

So we went to the second department store to visit its junior section. On the way there, we realized that we left the bag with the size four boy's clothes by the petites dressing room. I returned to the first store and received directions from my wife to find the junior section.

I went to where I thought she had told me to go, but I thought I must have gone to the wrong place. It seemed like I was in the lingerie section. Actually, it was more like a subsection of the lingerie section reserved for wedding night outfits and dresses for exotic dancers. I asked a young woman (who seemed entirely too young to be working in the red-light district of the department store) where the junior section was. She said, "Like duh, you're in it."

If you want to know why the teen pregnancy rate is so high, visit a junior clothing department.

With my sons, I was worried about finding clothes that seemed nice enough for church. With my teenage daughters I was worried about finding clothes that had enough material to avoid arrest for indecent exposure.

Aren't there enough people left in this country who attend church? Someone should start a mail-order business to sell nice, attractive church clothes. In the meantime, I can tell you where to buy clean bowling shirts. Bowling shirts are nicer than the T-shirts available for boys and are far more decent than any dress in the junior section.

How Can I Follow
If My Husband
Won't Lead?

Homeschooling moms often show up alone when I teach a seminar for fathers. They ask me questions about how to motivate their husbands. At times they express real frustration when their husbands seem spiritually disengaged. Many ask me for some form of a magic solution to convert their husbands into great spiritual leaders.

Is there an answer?

I approach this subject with a bit of trepidation. My goal is to encourage wives. My fear is that my discussions might actually serve to stir up bitter feelings by some wives against their husbands. God forbid such a result.

For years I have been encouraging fathers, especially homeschooling fathers, to be better spiritual leaders in their homes. The best method for me to encourage a wife is to communicate effectively this need to her husband. This is the core purpose of my book *The Homeschooling Father*.

As I confess in that book, I have not been the model spiritual leader. It is something I desire to be but something that is difficult to be consistently at the level that I would desire. I have improved over the years, but I strive to be better (and know that there is still plenty of room for growth).

Even if their husbands were not perfect in this area, most wives would be content if their husbands valued the goal of spiritual leadership, would make efforts in the right direction, and showed some improvement over time.

With all these caveats and disclaimers, let's face a sorrowful truth: Far too many husbands are not even on the path toward being a mature spiritual leader in their home. Some men never pray with their wife or their family. Some men never open the Word with their family. Some rarely go to church. And these are the professing Christians.

Other women are married to men who make no pretense of the Christian faith. They never go to church and are completely disinterested in spiritual things. A few are married to men who embrace a false religion of some stripe. Others are married to atheists, some with open bitterness to God and Jesus, His Son.

What are wives supposed to do in these situations? How do they make up for their husbands' neglect of this important role in the family's life?

Reread the last two sentences before you go on. OK, now focus with me. There is a biblical and proper answer to the first question. Wives are not left without hope when husbands refuse to be spiritual leaders. But there is no answer to the second question other than "You can't make up for your husband's failure to lead."

Read on for a minute before you react to what I just said.

There are ways for wives to react, cope, and improve in these circumstances. But there is no godly path by which the wife becomes the substitute spiritual leader of her home. You cannot fix the problem by attempting to do your husband's job of leading the home. If you try, you are probably interfering with God's pressure on your husband to urge him to do the right thing.

(I need to give the reader a caveat right now that flows from the fact that I am active in politics. There are people who read everything I write to try to find a basis for attacking me politically. We are about to embark on a lengthy discussion that assumes that it is a good thing for a wife to be submissive to her husband, as the New Testament teaches in Ephesians 5:22–24. No one requires a wife to believe the Bible. That is a free and voluntary act. I am writing to women who believe the Bible and want to follow what it says in every area of life including this one. It is unthinkable to me to enact the teaching of Ephesians 5 into the civil law of the United States. Feminists want to push their philosophy of life into the law in a way that takes the rights and lives of others—abortion taking the life of the unborn child being the chief example. But the vast majority of Christians reject the notion of using the government in this way. If you don't believe in the principles of Ephesians 5, you are not going to agree with the rest of this chapter. Fine. No one forces you to follow God. That is up to you.)

Before we do a step-by-step analysis of the issue of a woman's response when her husband won't lead, let's consider an example that hits very close to home for homeschooling moms, to illustrate the general principles involved.

A mom believes that God is directing her, through the Bible, to homeschool her children. Her husband disagrees and wants the children to attend public schools. What should she do?

First, and on every step of the way, she should pray. God is more concerned about the spiritual well-being of her children than she is, though at times it is hard to imagine how even God can care more than a mother does about her children.

A mom should be careful in her attitude, even in prayer in such a situation. It creates potential spiritual issues for the mom if her only prayer is that God would cause her husband to allow her to homeschool. She can certainly tell God that she would like that outcome. But the center of her prayer should be this: God, please move the heart of my husband to follow Your will for my children.

She should persist in such prayer. She should not be afraid to come to God time and time again on the same issue. How can she be confident that God won't think that a mom is whining in such a situation? Several passages of Scripture strongly encourage such praying. Consider three of them:

Luke 18:1–8

The first passage is one of my favorites, the parable of the persistent widow:

> Then Jesus told his disciples a parable to show them that they should always pray and not give up. He said: "In a certain town there was a judge who neither feared God nor cared about men. And there was a widow in that town who kept coming to him with the plea, 'Grant me justice against my adversary.'

"For some time he refused. But finally he said to himself, 'Even though I don't fear God or care about men, yet because this widow keeps bothering me, I will see that she gets justice, so that she won't eventually wear me out with her coming!'"

And the Lord said, "Listen to what the unjust judge says. And will not God bring about justice for his chosen ones, who cry out to him day and night? Will he keep putting them off? I tell you, he will see that they get justice, and quickly. However, when the Son of Man comes, will he find faith on the earth?"

Luke 11:5–13

A second passage from the New Testament follows the most famous of all prayers, the Lord's Prayer. The disciples asked Jesus to teach them to pray. He first taught them the Lord's Prayer, then He said this immediately afterward:

Then he said to them, "Suppose one of you has a friend, and he goes to him at midnight and says, 'Friend, lend me three loaves of bread, because a friend of mine on a journey has come to me, and I have nothing to set before him.'

"Then the one inside answers, 'Don't bother me. The door is already locked, and my children are with me in bed. I can't get up and give you anything.' I tell you, though he will not get up and give him the bread because he is his friend, yet because of the man's boldness he will get up and give him as much as he needs.

"So I say to you: Ask and it will be given to you; seek and you will find; knock and the door will be opened to you. For everyone who asks receives; he who seeks finds; and to him who knocks, the door will be opened.

"Which of you fathers, if your son asks for a fish, will give him a snake instead? Or if he asks for an egg, will give him a scorpion? If you then, though you are evil, know how to give good gifts to your children, how much more will your Father in heaven give the Holy Spirit to those who ask him!"

Isaiah 62:6–7

The third passage is from Isaiah's prophecy. This passage should drive home Jesus' point in the second passage:

I have posted watchmen on your walls, O Jerusalem;
they will never be silent day or night.
You who call on the LORD,
give yourselves no rest,
and give him no rest till he establishes Jerusalem
and makes her the praise of the earth.

Notice the two components of what God tells us to do when we are trying to build up our "Jerusalem," our spiritual heritage in the lives of our children. One is to give ourselves no rest. In other words, we should be persistent in our efforts to do those things that we know to do to accomplish God's purposes in our lives.

But the other idea is remarkable in its wording: We should give God no rest either. A mother should be bold to persist in praying that God would move through her husband to give him the plan that God has for her family.

A mom should not think that "giving him no rest" is a good tactic to be applied to her husband. It is fine—in fact, it is essentially mandatory—for a husband and wife to have a series of serious talks about a subject that is as important as the education of their children. A wife should strive to tell her husband her heart on the matter. A husband's responsibility is to listen well and understand, but that is his responsibility, not his wife's. It is not a sign that he does not understand simply because he disagrees.

A wife should ask her husband to help her understand his position regarding homeschooling. Why does he oppose it? What goals does he have for the children? What are his priorities for them?

In the preliminary stages it is fine for a wife to do some research and give answers to her husband's questions on the subject. She can also attempt to show that homeschooling is consistent with his goals and his priorities for the children. But she should not continue this at length. It is fine for a wife to say: "I accept your decision about priorities and goals. Is it OK if I try to put together some information to show you that homeschooling meets your priorities and goals?" It is inappropriate for a wife to keep going on and on about a subject, because both of them know at some point that she does not really accept her husband's decisions about goals and priorities and that she is just trying to get her own way.

If a wife has shared her heart, asked her husband for his goals and priorities, tried to show him that homeschooling meets his standards, and he still disagrees, it is time for them to leave the subject alone and for the wife to follow her husband's decision.

It is perfectly acceptable for the wife to continue petitioning her Heavenly Father on the issue—to give Him no rest. But even in that it is very important that she not develop the heart attitude, "My husband is wrong, God; please fix him." The prayer should continue to be, "God, please move through my husband. Please, give me contentment to follow."

Now, let's step back from the particular example and look at the subject in more general terms.

The issue is what should a wife do if her husband won't lead.

Step 1: Deciding If He Isn't Leading or If You Just Don't Like His Decision

In the lengthy example we just considered, the husband made a clear decision: he wanted the children to attend public schools. He was leading. His reasoning did not satisfy his wife. He may not have used principles from the Bible to make his decision. But he was leading. He made a decision. He was clear.

A wife who simply doesn't like her husband's decision needs to find contentment not resentment. She can continue to pour out her heart to God. But she must be very careful if she continually pours out her heart to her friends on the issue. She will be tempted to resent her husband and to be reinforced in that resentment when her friends say, "Oh, how can you stand it when he is so wrong?" If you told me the situation, I might be thinking, *Your husband is sure being foolish about this.* But woe unto me if I should say such a thing. You need to avoid situations and people that put you on the path of resentment.

Here is the big truth. For your husband to be the spiritual leader you desire him to be, you have to be truly willing to follow.

I have been in marital counseling situations where the wife says essentially, "I am quite willing to follow my husband except when he is wrong." (Please leave aside the rare situations where a husband asks a wife to do something that is morally or legally wrong such as joining him in cheating on their income taxes. We will return to these situations a little later.) The real test of being submissive is being willing to follow her husband when a wife thinks he is making the wrong decision.

If a woman desires to have a husband who is a true spiritual leader, her first priority is to be a true spiritual follower.

Consider the hypothetical case of seventeen-year-old Josh. His parents want him to be home by 11 P.M. on weeknights and midnight on weekends. He continually comes home later than this. His parents ground him, but he sneaks out when they go to bed. They take away his privileges, and it just doesn't work. He continues to argue with them about the curfew they set, and he gets around it every chance he gets. He simply will not truly acquiesce to his parents' decision.

After a while, a parent simply gives up in a situation like that. You may have to tell your son to move out of the house, but that is a really big decision, and you are probably unwilling to do that until pushed to the limit. When you have a seventeen-year-old who simply will not agree with your decision, you are not failing to lead him. He is failing to follow. After a while, it may feel to him like you are no longer leading. But the reality is that the rule was made, and it is still there for him to follow. He has to return into the sphere of your authority in order for leading and following to make any sense.

I hope you get the analogy. Many men were once willing to lead their wives. But after constant resistance, they have just given up. It is just too big of a hassle every time they try to make a decision, so they stop. They don't want to lose their marriage over the issue, so they quit leading.

Now, let me be careful to say that I think the extreme form of this situation is rare. Very few men refuse to be the spiritual leaders that God wants them to be solely because of the pattern of their wife's resistance. But this pattern is present very often *to some degree* in marriages where the wife is unhappy that her husband won't provide spiritual leadership.

Mom, if you feel the conviction of the Holy Spirit resting on your soul at this moment, here is what you should do if you truly want your husband to become a spiritual leader who follows God. Go to him right now and tell him that you have been wrong in resisting his leadership. Cite a few examples if God brings them to mind. Ask him to forgive you for resisting him. Tell him that with God's help you will try to do your best to follow him willingly in the future.

I know that this will be extraordinarily hard. Your mind will be thinking, *But what if he makes a morally abusive decision and I have just promised to follow him?* Don't get sidetracked by such thoughts. You are promising to follow with the assumption that your husband will act in good faith. If someday he says, "All right, you promised to follow, so I want you to join me in a wife-swapping club," you can tell him absolutely not. Don't let your willingness to get things right with your husband be wrecked by fear that he might abuse the rights of leadership. If it is true abuse (that is, if he demands that you do something illegal, immoral, or unhealthy), then that is a completely different situation. Just assume that he will be normal and go talk to him.

When you are truly willing to follow your husband, even when you think he is wrong, you are on the first step toward contentment for you. That is the most important thing you can gain out of the situation. Your decision may prompt him to be a better leader. But even if this doesn't happen right away (or ever), you have gained contentment, which is to be highly prized.

Step 2: Learning to Talk It Out

One of the most frustrating things for a wife is to have hopes and desires for spiritual leadership that go unmet. One of the most frustrating things for her husband is not to know about those hopes and desires.

The church at large has failed Christian men in this area. We are told that we should be spiritual leaders but given little practical instruction on how to implement this duty. We know we should take our families to church. We know we should pray for our families. We know we should do family devotions, but most of us receive little instruction from our churches to help us carry out this responsibility. (I deal with the dad's side of this in chapter 1 of *The Homeschooling Father.*)

A wife can accomplish two things by sharing with her husband the details of her hopes and desires for spiritual leadership. First, *her husband might actually learn something that helps him assume spiritual leadership.* A wife might have some very practical suggestions that help her husband figure out a plan to improve his leadership that has been stymied, not for lack of desire, but for lack of practical plans for implementation.

She might say, "It would really mean a lot to me if you would read a chapter from the Bible to our family after dinner." That kind of statement of hopes and dreams might well spark your husband into action.

The second even more important reason for sharing your hopes and dreams with your husband is this: *He might learn how important this is to his wife.*

About twelve years ago, I stumbled into Vickie's prayer journal. She writes very small and conserves paper, so this one notebook covered several years of weekly prayer requests. At the start of the journal, the number one request every week was, "Make Mike a better spiritual leader in our home." It really hit me hard.

As I paged through the months and years that followed that request, I noticed that this request started appearing lower and lower on her weekly list. I asked her if my lower ranking meant that I was improving. She said (and I am translating loosely), "You may be improving, but you are not off the list."

I can tell you for sure that knowing how important this was to Vickie really motivated me to want to do better. She had said things to me from time to time, so I can't say that I didn't know that she prized this. But there was something about knowing how much she prized this that made me want to do better than before.

Mom, your husband may be more willing than you know to pick up the pace of spiritual leadership if he learns from your heart how important this is to you.

I believe it is really important for you to understand the critical difference between sharing your heart and complaining. Most women are more than smart enough to understand this distinction in intellectual terms. However, there is an emotional component of this that is a bit trickier. Remember that your goal is to be content before God in this matter. If you are willing to be content, no matter how disappointed you may be for the moment, you probably can avoid the pitfall of complaining when you intend just to "share your heart."

Don't get me wrong about complaining. I am not saying that complaining is not justified in some cases. I am certainly not saying that your husband is perfect. He's not Jesus, so I know he's not perfect. Nonetheless, there are two key reasons why complaining defeats the very goal you are trying to reach—that is, letting your husband know how important his spiritual leadership is to you.

First, a complainer is attempting to take control of the situation. A complainer is demanding a solution. There are times when, as consumers, we need to complain. We need to make demands and take control. But if you want your husband to become the spiritual leader of your home, taking control of the situation and making demands is leading you in the exact opposite direction to the one that you both need to be going.

Second, becoming a complainer drags you away from the key to your joy—that is, contentment. You may have joy, even if your husband fails miserably at spiritual leadership, but you will have to be extraordinarily careful to place the goal of contentment as your highest emotional priority.

Share your heart. Tell your husband how much his spiritual leadership would mean to you. Give him some insight on how you think this would benefit your children. The vast majority of men will be moved by such deep sharing from the heart of the woman they love.

Step 3: Appeal

You've prayed. You've shared your heart. You've continued to pray. You've waited patiently and nothing has happened. You still don't pray together as a couple. Your family never has times of reading and learning from God's Word together. Your husband shows no particular interest in the spiritual welfare of your children. What do you do now?

Although my steps of action so far have assumed that your husband is a professing Christian, much of what I have said is applicable even if he isn't. But how should you proceed if your husband doesn't profess faith in Christ?

If your husband does not profess a personal relationship with Christ and rejects your efforts to encourage him in that direction, you should take counsel from 1 Peter 3:1–6, a passage of Scripture that speaks directly to your situation.

> Wives, in the same way be submissive to your husbands so that, if any of them do not believe the word, they may be won over without words by the behavior of their wives, when they see the purity and reverence of your lives. Your beauty should not come from outward adornment, such as braided hair and the wearing of gold jewelry and fine clothes. Instead, it should be that of your inner self, the unfading beauty of a gentle and quiet spirit, which is of great worth in God's sight. For this is the way the holy women of the past who put their hope in God used to make themselves beautiful. They were submissive to their own husbands, like Sarah, who obeyed Abraham and called him her master. You are her daughters if you do what is right and do not give way to fear.

Your goal is to win your husband. There is only one way to win him. It will never work to beat him down with a stream of constant arguments or requests. Scripture says win him over with quiet beauty from your inner self. That requires you to be beautiful on the inside. Contentment, my constant theme, is the key to such beauty. Pray persistently, be gentle and loving, and ask God to fulfill the implied promise in this passage for you.

So what about the woman married to the professing believer? There are two passages of Scripture for you. The first is the same one we just read from 1 Peter. This passage is written to women whose husbands "don't believe the Word." Unbelievers don't believe the Word at all. Men who are professing Christians but who refuse to be spiritual leaders in their homes don't believe that part of the Word that urges them to be the spiritual leader of their wife and children. The approach of 1 Peter can work in either situation. A woman who wants her husband to truly believe the Word and apply it has the hope that comes from loving her husband with quiet inner beauty. It is a selfless approach. But as is so often the case in the Christian life, the selfless path is the most powerful.

First Peter instructs you to make a quiet appeal. You become appealing to your husband, while appealing in prayer to your Heavenly Father.

For women married to believers, we also need to consider Matthew 18:15–17:

"If your brother sins against you, go and show him his fault, just between the two of you. If he listens to you, you have won your brother over. But if he will not listen, take one or two others along, so that 'every matter may be established by the testimony of two or three witnesses.' If he refuses to listen to them, tell it to the church; and if he refuses to listen even to the church, treat him as you would a pagan or a tax collector."

When can a wife appeal a decision or practice of her husband using the principle of Matthew 18?

Recently, I heard of a situation where a woman went to the elders in her church without her husband's knowledge. Her complaint was that he was failing to lead the family in devotions and generally lacked the other attributes of spiritual leadership. When her husband heard about this, it placed a serious strain on their marriage. He felt betrayed, because his wife, in his opinion, had gone behind his back to the elders in a way that embarrassed him.

How do we apply Matthew 18 in the context of a marriage between two believers?

First of all, notice what triggers the application of Matthew 18. It requires your brother to sin against you. There is a critical distinction between your husband sinning against you and disappointing you. *There is no basis for invoking Matthew 18 if all that has happened is that your husband has disappointed you and failed to fulfill your desires and expectations.*

Here is where the immoral, illegal, or unhealthy requests of a husband can be appealed. If your husband asks you to cheat on your taxes or violate some clear moral command of the Word of God or does something that compromises your health or safety, then he has sinned against you. If you resist and this becomes a point of contention, then you may well need to go to your church leaders or to appropriate family members (his father, for example) and appeal. If he simply makes an improper demand and you say no and he leaves it alone, then you should leave it alone as well.

The failure to be a spiritual leader in the home is a failure of the duty of the husband. But I cannot say, at least in the normal range of these kinds of failures, that a husband's neglect of this duty constitutes a sin against the wife.

All husbands and wives commit many sins against each other on a regular basis. We are rude, thoughtless, selfish, prideful, angry, and unloving. If you go running off to your elders every time your husband sins against you, they will get very tired of hearing from you, and it will ruin your marriage. (Keep in mind that he could run off and complain to them every time you sin as well, and you certainly wouldn't like that.)

The general rule in marriage is this: "Above all, love each other deeply, because love covers over a multitude of sins" (1 Peter 4:8).

But there comes a point where sin disrupts homes. This may result from repeated sin. But some sins, adultery, for example, can disrupt a marriage even when done only once or twice. They go across the line, and the wife truly needs to take the steps outlined in Matthew 18. This act could damage her marriage, so she must be certain that the circumstances warrant such action before proceeding.

The second step of Matthew 18 involves bringing two or three others along to hear the two of you discuss the matter. Their role is to help each of you see the truth. In theory, they should be able to say you are wrong or that your husband is wrong, depending on what they find.

Let me sound one additional caution in all of this. Unless you are in a situation where you are in some realistic danger, I think that it is imperative that you take the second step in the Matthew 18 process only with your husband's advance knowledge. Ask him if he is willing to go have a talk with the elders to get some help in resolving the dispute. It is far better when you have his agreement to go together to see two or three elders (or some other spiritually appropriate individuals you have selected together).

If the Bible gives us this process, why should you want to seek your husband's agreement to go? Your goal is to reconcile a conflict. It is a whole lot easier to reach reconciliation when there is an up-front agreement to enter into that process.

Again, if you or your children are in danger, go alone. Get help. But if it is some other kind of conflict, you are miles ahead when your husband agrees in advance to go with you.

The goal of the appeal is to have God's will and His Word honored in the situation. That is the standard by which we must live out our faith. If your goal is simply to get your way, you will undoubtedly be disappointed. You need to be committed to God's outcome of the appeal, keeping in mind that elders can really only exercise moral authority over either of you. There is no one to coerce anybody to follow the outcome of a Matthew 18 appeal. Unless God convicts the heart, any sort of human intervention will be rejected by a resistant spouse.

Step 4: What Then?

You have expressed your willingness to follow. You have sought forgiveness for any past resistance. You have prayed. You have persisted in prayer. You have shared your heart. And, if appropriate, you have appealed. Still he does nothing. What then?

This is when you simply have to trust God. First Peter 3 teaches you to win with quiet inner beauty. There is a clear implication that you love your husband with all your heart despite his complete or partial rejection of the Word of God.

It may take years for you to win your husband using the tactic of quiet inner beauty. He may never change. But how can you lose when you have practiced the art of inner beauty during all these years? Your contentment, your joy, and your attractiveness to your husband will grow and grow. He is responsible for himself. You cannot be the Holy Spirit in his life. You are only responsible for yourself. You are a winner when you practice quiet beauty if only in the area of your own inner peace. Winning that battle is worth a mountain of diamonds.

Practical Questions of Detail

If my husband won't teach the Bible to our family, should I?

Yes. You cannot be a substitute for your husband's leadership, but Scripture assumes that a mother will teach her children (Proverbs 1:8, 6:20). God directs parents to teach their children to love God and obey His commands (Deuteronomy 6).

However, I would strongly suggest that you do such teaching in a way that does not appear confrontational or to be a substitute for your husband. Don't take out the family Bible after dinner and start teaching in front of your husband. Since you are home-schooling, the setting is perfect. Begin your school day with a time of teaching and application from God's Word that is appropriate for your children.

Should I take my children to church alone?

By all means. If your husband doesn't forbid you, then the issue is easy. Take them to church. If he forbids you from taking the children to church, then you probably need to follow his directions in this. Teach them at home. If he doesn't forbid playing sermon tapes, do that instead.

But what if he takes them to the house of worship of a false religion?

This is the most difficult issue of all for me. But I think you need to follow the example of Moses's mother. Her son was taken into the house of Pharaoh. We should assume that he was exposed to the education, philosophy, and religion of the Pharaohs. Moses's mother undoubtedly prayed for her son and taught him the truth whenever she could. You should do the same. A mom should do everything in her power to protect her children in such circumstances, but asking God to protect them is the last line of defense when your unbelieving husband insists.

Do I have to go with my husband to a house of worship for a false religion?

No. But make sure you are talking about a clearly false religion and not a denominational dispute between varieties of churches that essentially teach the fundamental truths of the Christian faith.

When it comes to ordering you to worship a false god, your husband crosses the line. For this, the words of Acts 5:29 are applicable: "Peter and the other apostles replied: 'We must obey God rather than men!'"

Remember that this entire chapter was written to women who already agree with the Bible's teaching that a wife should submit to her husband's leadership. But no man, including a husband, has the authority to order a woman to disobey God. Although it is never a joyous occasion to be called to decide between loyalty to a husband's wishes and the commands of God, always obey God.

Conclusion

If your husband won't lead, you can and should pray for him. But his lack of response should never stop you from following God. Follow God. Seek contentment. Gain the joy that no man can steal.